T0278078

ENCHANTED WALES

Enchanted Wales

Myth and Magic in Welsh Storytelling

Miranda Aldhouse-Green

with illustrations by Jacob Stead

2023

www.uwp.co.uk

British Library Cataloguing-in-Publication Data
A catalogue record for this book is available from the British Library.

ISBN: 978-1-915279-18-7

Pronunciation Guide by Anwen Hayward
Cover artwork by Andy Ward
Map and illustrations by Jacob Stead
Typeset by Agnes Graves
Printed by CPI Group (UK) Ltd, Croydon CR0 4YY

The publisher acknowledges the financial support of the Books Council of Wales.

*I dedicate this book to the people of Wales
and to the memory of my sister, Juliet Gordon*

Away with us he's going
The solemn-eyed:
He'll hear no more the lowing
Of the calves on the warm hillside
Or the kettle on the hob
Sing peace into his breast
Or see the brown mice bob
Round and round the oatmeal-chest.
*For he comes, the human child,
To the waters and the wild
With a faery, hand in hand,
From a world more full of weeping than he can understand.*

From W. B. Yeats, 'The Stolen Child'

CILGWRI

ABERFFRAW ABER
          SAINT
ABER   LLANRWST
MENAI   (CWM CAWLWYD)*
                              FARNDON
                              (RHEDENFRE)*

GWERNABWY   TRAWSFYNYDD
          HARLECH

PORTH
CERDDIN   HEREFORD

          NARBERTH   GLOUCESTER
          (ARBERTH)   (CAER LOYW)
GRASSHOLM
(GWALES)   CAERLEON
                LLYN LLIW GWENT-
                           IS-COED

                              N
                         W ✦ E
                              S

*POSSIBLE MODERN-DAY LOCATION

Contents

Pronunciation Guide
to Welsh Names and Places
By Anwen Hayward

✳

Welsh may look daunting at first, but in fact it is much easier to pronounce than it may appear at a glance. Welsh is a phonetic language, meaning that each letter is pronounced consistently, with no silent letters. Subsequently, almost every word can be read aloud on sight once the alphabet is learnt. As a general rule, emphasis falls on the penultimate syllable in each word.

Welsh consonants

The following consonants are pronounced the same way in Welsh as in English: *b, d, h, l, m, n, p, t.* Some letters are written as digraphs, meaning that two characters are used to represent one sound, e.g. *ff, ng, dd* – these are all considered single letters, and are pronounced differently to *f, n, g* and *d*.

c	always hard, as in *cat*, and never soft, as in *mice*
ch	an aspirated *c* sound, like the Scottish *loch*
dd	a voiced *th*, as in the English *the*
f	like an English *v*, as in *dove*
ff	like an English *f*, as in *four*
g	always hard, as in *glove*, never soft, as in *gem*
ng	always hard, as in *finger*, never soft, as in *angel*
ll	this digraph does not have an English equivalent sound, but is pronounced by pressing the tongue to the roof of the mouth and gently blowing air around the tongue to make an aspirated sound. The closest English equivalent would be something similar to the 'cl' in 'clan', although this is only loosely approximate

r	always trilled, as in Spanish or Italian, or as pronounced in a Scottish accent
s	always sibilant, as in *snow*, never voiced, as in *rose*
rh	an aspirated *r*, best made by exhaling and trilling an *r* sound
th	an unvoiced *th*, as in the English *think*, never as in *the*

Vowels

Vowels in Welsh have both short and long pronunciations, with short forms as follows.

a	as in *cat*	*i*	as in *pig*	*w*	as in *loot*
e	as in *met*	*o*	as in *fog*	*y*	as in *dull*
		u	as in *peek*		

Diphthongs

Diphthongs are pairs of vowels which are pronounced as a single syllable.

ae, ai, au	as in *eye*	*iw, yw*	as in *stew*
aw	as in *cow*	*oe, oi*	as in *oil*
ei, eu, ey	as in *pay*	*ow*	as in *go*
ew	*eh+ooh*, said quickly so that each sound glides into the other	*wy*	*ooh+ee*, said quickly so that each sound glides into the other

Pronouncing the Mabinogion

Note that due to the lack of an equivalent for the Welsh *ll*, whenever *ll* appears in the list below, it signifies that the Welsh *ll* should be used. The same applies to *ch*, *dd* and *rh*, which should always be pronounced as above. Capital letters indicate stress.

Aberffraw: ah-ber-FFROW	**Aber Saint:** AH-ber SIGN-t
Aber Menai: AH-ber MEN-eye	**Afagddu:** ah-VAG-ddee [Welsh *dd*]

Annwfn: ann-OOV-un

Aranrhod: ah-RAN-rhod [Welsh *rh*]

Arawn: AR-own [to rhyme with *frown*]

Arberth: ARR-bear-th

Bendigeidfran: ben-dee-GADE-vran

Blodeuwedd: blod-AY-wedd [Welsh *dd,* AY to rhyme with *pay*]

Bleiddwn: BLAY-ddoon [Welsh *dd*]

Brân: br-AAH-n [note that the circumflex indicates a long *a* sound]

Branwen: BRAN-wen

Caerleon: k-eye-r-LAY-on

Caer Loyw: K-EYE-r LOY-oo

Caerwent: K-EYE-r-went

Cei: KAY

Ceridwen: ker-ID-wen

Cigfa: KEEG-vah

Cilgwri: kil-GOO-ree

Cilydd: KIL-idd [Welsh *dd*]

Crearwy: kray-AR-ooy

Culhwch: KUL-ooch [Welsh *ch*]

Cwm Cawlwyd: KOOM KOW-looyd

cwn Annwfn: koon ann-OOV-un

Derwedd: DERR-wedd [Welsh *dd*]

Diwrnach: DEW-r-nach [Welsh *ch*]

Dôn: DAWN

Drudwyn: DREED-ooen

Dylan: DUH-lan

Efnisien: ev-NEES-ee-en

Efrog: EV-rog

Englyn: ENG-lin

Gilfaethwy: gil-VYE-thooy

Goewin: GOI-win

Gofannon: gov-ANNE-on

Goleuddydd: gol-AY-ddidd [Welsh *dd*]

Gorsedd: GORR-sedd [Welsh *dd*]

Gronw: GRON-oo

Grugyn Gwrych Eraint: GREEG-in GOO-rich ER-eye-nt [Welsh *ch*]

Gwales: GWAH-less

Gwawl: goo-OWL

Gwent-Is Coed: GWENT-EES COY-d

Gwern: goo-ERN

Gwernabwy: goo-ern-AB-ooy

Gwion: GWEE-on

Gwrhyr: GOO-r-HEER [Welsh *rh*]

Gwyddbwyll: goo-EEDD-booy-ll [Welsh *dd* and *ll*]

Gwydion: GOOyd-eeon

Gwynedd: GWIN-edd [Welsh *dd*]

Hafgan: HAV-gan

Harlech: HAR-lech

Hychdwn Hir: HUCH-doon HEER

Hyddwn: HUH-ddoon [Welsh *dd*]

Hyfaidd: HUV-aye-dd [Welsh *dd*]

Hywel Dda: HUH-wel DDA [Welsh *dd*]

Llanrwst: llan-ROOST [Welsh *ll*]

Lleu Llaw Gyffes: LLAY LLOW guh-FESS [Welsh *ll*]

Llŷn (Peninsula): LLEEN [Welsh *ll*]

Llyn Cerrig Bach: LLIN KER-ig BAH-ch [Welsh *ll*]

Llyn Fawr: LLIN VOW-r [Welsh *ll*]

Llyn Llyw: LLIN LLEW [rhymes with *stew*] [Welsh *ll*]

Llŷr: LLEER [Welsh *ll*]

Mabinogi: mab-in-OG-ee

Mabinogion: mab-in-OG-ee-on

Mabon: MAB-on

Macsen Wledig: MAK-sen oo-LED-ig

Manawydan: man-ah-WUH-dan

Math: MATH

Matholwch: math-OL-ooch [Welsh *ch*]

Mesur-y-Peir: MESS-eer-uh-pAYE-r

Modron: MOD-ron

Moel Hiraddug: moyle here-AH-ddig [Welsh *dd*]

Nisien: NEES-ee-en

Olwen: OL-wen

Owain: OH-wine

Peredur: per-ED-eer

Porth Cerddin: POR-th KER-ddin [Welsh *dd*]

Preiddeu Annwfn: PRAY-dday ann-OOV-un [Welsh *dd*]

Pryderi: pruh-DERRY

Pwyll: POOY-ll

Rhedynfre: rheh-DONE-vre [Welsh *rh*]

Rhiannon: rhee-ANNE-on [Welsh *rh*]

Rhonabwy: rhon-AB-ooy [Welsh *rh*]

Rhydderch: RHUH-dd-ERR-ch [Welsh *rh* and *dd*]

Taliesin: tal-YES-in

Teyrnon: TAY-r-non

Trawsfynydd: trows-VUN-idd [Welsh *dd*]

Trioedd Ynys Prydein: TREE-oydd UN-iss PRUD-ey-n

Twrch Trwyth: TOO-r-ch TROOY-th

Urien: IR-ee-en

Ysbaddaden: us-badd-AD-en [Welsh *dd*]

Cei and Gwrhyr ride the Salmon of Llyn Llyw
to the fortress of Caer Loyw.

Myths and Mythmakers

What are myths and what purpose do they serve? These are complicated questions that require considered answers. Myths are stories that explore issues central to, but also beyond, human comprehension; and they are frequently tales inhabited by supernatural, 'contra-normal' beings and occurrences that are shot through with magic. In myths, as in dreams, reality is suspended and literally anything can happen. There are no boundaries. In myths, as in fairy tales, the nub of the story is often associated with the conflict between right and wrong. Take the well-known tale of 'Little Red Riding Hood', as an example. In this story, we encounter themes that are echoed in many mythic traditions: shape-shifting (or skin-turning), and a confrontation between an innocent child or personification of ordered humanity, and the villainous representative of untamed evil. So the 'baddy', the wild wolf (having devoured Red Riding Hood's grandmother) dresses up as his victim in order to deceive and consume his opposite: a powerless little girl.

But myths are so much more than fairy tales. Myths allow people to explore the darkest aspects of human nature within a safe environment (around a campfire, for example). A central function of myths is to attempt to explain the inexplicable: what it means to be human and how humanity fits into the wider world of risk, threat and 'otherness', including the spirit world. Mythic tales can address fundamental questions for people. How was the world created? How did we come into being? How did we get here? What happens when we die? How are the cycles of day and night and the seasons to be explained? Issues around the human condition are explored and explained in mythic tales: good and evil, war and peace, gender and fertility, life and death, and life *after* death.

Myths typically flourished within simpler, less factually informed societies, where a combination of the absence of scientific knowledge and non-literacy combined to create the perfect environment for them. The lack of written testimony is key to understanding how Welsh myths (alongside their Irish cousins) were transmitted between individuals and communities. In Wales in particular, where my interests lie, these 'supernatural' stories began their lives within the medium of oral tradition. They were tales told by professional storytellers who travelled from court to court and between far-flung communities, entertaining and bringing information. They would adapt their narratives to include news and introduce fresh topics in order, perhaps, to flatter the inhabitants of particular noble houses who gathered to hear the latest gossip and to listen to strange tales. The medium of the spoken word is especially powerful. It is possible to imagine the storyteller adopting different voices for different characters, or even several storytellers taking part in what would have turned into almost theatrical presentations.

And so we come to a set of crucial questions: when were the seeds of the Welsh mythic oral tradition sown? And when – and in what context – were these stories written down? The origins of the Welsh myths will always remain hidden in the mists of antiquity. But it is fair to say that their beginnings probably lie in the deep past, maybe more than a millennium before they were enshrined within literature. That the tales have their foundations in oral storytelling is indubitably evident in telltale 'footprints' like the clearly episodic nature of the narratives which had breaks in the texts at specific, emotive stages, designed – just as in modern television soaps – to keep the audience on tenterhooks for the next instalment.

It is possible to trace the written origins of Welsh mythology to medieval times, as we will see in later chapters. However – and this is a contentious issue, hotly denounced or at least questioned by some historians – it is my belief that at least some medieval mythic narratives may have drawn inspiration from the remote past as far back as the Iron Age and Roman Welsh culture. The evidence for such beginnings rests upon some very distinct points of reference, where certain themes within the literature chime loudly with earlier archaeological evidence. As an example, we will meet the divine 'heroine', Rhiannon, who is inextricably identified with horses and is featured in two out of the Four Branches of the *Mabinogion*. Gallo-Roman and Romano-British communities worshipped a horse-goddess, named on inscriptions as 'Epona' (an ancient Gallo-British word referring to horses), and depicted in iconography as a woman seated side-saddle on a mare or enthroned and flanked by two ponies. In attempting to argue how links between the ancient Irish/British/Welsh past and the medieval mythic texts may have come about, one possible model may be found in the bridging periods of the sixth and seventh centuries AD, when early Christian saints issued from monasteries and roamed Britain and Europe in sacred journeys known as the *peregrinationes pro Dei amore* (pilgrimages for the love of God). Could it not be that such travelling clerics encountered images and inscribed stones relating to the worship of Epona, and wove them into their stories that were handed down and later became embedded within medieval mythic texts?

A striking thing about the medievally recorded myths (whatever form their oral roots might have taken) is the context within which they were committed to writing: by Christian monks in monasteries, as was Irish mythic literature. But there is a huge religious difference between the Irish and Welsh material. The earliest Irish narratives date from the eighth century AD, and are riddled with paganism. Gods and goddesses stalk through the stories, with nary a mention of Christianity, despite the myths being recorded within the context of early Irish Christian religious foundations. However, the Welsh myths were written down centuries later, most of them not until the thirteenth or fourteenth centuries, and they contain multiple, if somewhat elliptical, allusions to the Christian God (as opposed to the gods). The supernatural beings are 'watered-down'. They are presented, perhaps, as demoted divine beings, and certainly not as full-fleshed deities. Perhaps this is due, in part at least, to the fact that they were recorded later in writing. Nevertheless, both the Welsh and Irish myths are overflowing with elements that promote Christian values: chastity, honesty and the ills associated with warfare.

So, come with me on a journey to explore the fascinating collection of Welsh mythological texts. These are stories that are heavy with magic, monsters and the supernatural; severed heads that are still alive; talking beasts; capricious cauldrons; shape-shifters; magical mounds, spells, witches and wizards and so much more. Welcome to the 'Narnia' of enchanted Wales.

CHAPTER I

Opening the Door on the Welsh Myths

'Lord,' said one of Pwyll's court, 'it is the peculiarity of the mound that whatever high-born man sits upon it will not go thence without one of two things: wounds or blows, or else his seeing a wonder.'

'I do not fear wounds or blows amidst such a host as this, but as to the wonder, I should be glad to see that. I will go', said he, 'to the mound, to sit.'

This quotation is taken from the First Branch of the *Mabinogi*, (better known as the *Mabinogion*). The Four Branches are a group of four principal tales in the collection of the eleven Welsh mythic tales that constitute the *Mabinogion*. Other important stories among these eleven tales include 'Peredur, son of Efrog', 'The Dream of the Emperor Macsen', '*Culhwch ac Olwen*' ('Culhwch and Olwen') and 'Rhonabwy's Dream'. The passage is a fine example of the way in which these myths were delivered before they were written down: partly because it clearly speaks with the voice of an oral storyteller, and also because it shows the speaker's wish to keep the audience's attention, by priming listeners to brace themselves for the weird and wonderful happenings ahead.

Pwyll, Lord of Arberth, hunts on horseback
with his white, red-eared hounds.

The reason why such a rich collection of Welsh mythology survives is because, sometime in the medieval period, between about AD 1000 and 1500, oral stories were set down in writing by monks working in monasteries, where the main skills of literacy were concentrated. The two principal collections of mythic stories are preserved in the *White Book of Rhydderch* and the *Red Book of Hergest*, the former put together around 1300 and the latter slightly later, during the fourteenth century. In this chapter, we shall mainly focus on the Four Branches, because of the richness and variety of the stories. But there are other important tales that we will explore along the way.

The Branches of the *Mabinogion* are standalone stories but also contain certain joining elements. For example, particular heroes or heroines appear in more than one Branch. So, for instance, Rhiannon (the horse-goddess) appears in both the First and the Third Branch, as does her son Pryderi. These stories are set mostly in south-west and north-west Wales, and centred around Narberth (Pembrokeshire) and Harlech (Gwynedd). The First Branch tells the story of Pwyll, Lord (*Llys*) of Arberth (which is the older name for the town now known as Narberth) and his wife Rhiannon. Like the other three Branches, it is shot through with weird happenings and strange beings.

Otherworlds: Pwyll and Arawn

We first encounter Pwyll, Lord of Arberth while he is out hunting in a forest with his pack of hounds. On this occasion, he and his entourage clashed with another hunter and his own pack of dogs. They quarrelled over a stag that the stranger's pack had downed but that Pwyll's dogs took over as their own kill. The stranger's name was Arawn and he was Lord of Annwfn, the otherworld – the King of the Dead. This dark lord struck a deal with Pwyll: the two were to change places for a year, so that Arawn would rule over Arberth, as Pwyll, and vice versa.

We don't learn much about how Arawn got on while masquerading as Pwyll; instead, the story shines a spotlight on Annwfn, the Welsh underworld, and on Pwyll's experiences there. Annwfn is described as a wonderful place – like the world of living humans but much better.

It was a land of feasting, music, dancing, hunting and game-playing. But Arawn also gave Pwyll an important task to fulfil while he reigned there: to kill a rival otherworld lord, Hafgan. He does so, and then returns to his own land after the year has passed. When Arawn returned to Annwfn, he discovered something interesting – and here I think the Christian value of chastity comes into play – for when he came to his wife's bed, he realised from her reaction that Pwyll had not had sexual intercourse with his wife.

Vanishing babies:
Rhiannon, lady of horses, and Pryderi

One day, when Pwyll was out with his followers, he came across the *Gorsedd Arberth*, the sacred mound hedged about with magic. Anyone who sat on this mound would have one of two things happen to him: either his body would be violently assaulted or he would have a wondrous vision. Pwyll chose to sit there, boasting that he was not afraid of any threats. And he did, indeed, see something magical: a fair lady clad in gold silk, riding a shimmering white horse. Pwyll was intrigued by the sight and told one of his horsemen to intercept her. But, however fast this man rode, he could not catch up with the lady, even though she seemed not to be riding at all swiftly. So Pwyll, himself, rode after the mysterious stranger but he could not overtake her either. In desperation, he called out to her and immediately she reined in her mount, stopped and spoke to him. She told him that she had been waiting for him to address her and that her name was Rhiannon. The two fell in love and agreed that they should meet again a year from then at the court of a nobleman called Hyfaidd, and get married. At the year's end, Pwyll set out with 100 riders for Hyfaidd's court, but there encountered a love-rival, called Gwawl. Rhiannon didn't want to wed this other man, and sought to conspire with Pwyll to avoid having to marry Gwawl. The ruse was successful and Rhiannon and Pwyll married, and lived contentedly for three years.

But Pwyll had done something dishonourable to win his bride. Gwawl had been Rhiannon's suitor prior to him and had declared his love for her first. The way things worked in those days meant that he should have been the one to marry her. Pwyll saw a way to cheat Gwawl by trickery. To win the hand of Rhiannon, one night during a feast at *Llys Arberth*, Pwyll persuaded Gwawl to place his feet into a magic bag, which had the property of infinite capacity. Gwawl became caught up in the bag, and his followers were treated similarly and trapped in other bags. And then, even more shamefully, Pwyll and his men played a kind of football game with the men-filled bags, which they called 'badger in the bag'. Gwawl and his trapped followers were released but only when they agreed to certain terms: these included Gwawl giving up any claim to Rhiannon.

At the end of the first three years of the couple's marriage, Pwyll's people began to grow restive because there was no sign of an heir, and they asked him to get rid of Rhiannon since she appeared to be barren. Pwyll was troubled and asked for a year's grace before deciding. And lo and behold, before the year's end, a son was born to the royal couple. But when the baby was only a day old, disaster struck. That night, the six women detailed to watch over him, as well as his mother, fell asleep. When they awoke, the baby had vanished. The watch-women were terrified and decided to cover up their careless guardianship by framing the baby's mother for his disappearance. So they killed a new-born puppy and smeared its blood over the sleeping Rhiannon's face and hands, so that it would look not only as though she'd murdered the child, but that she had partially eaten him.

Convinced of Rhiannon's guilt, Pwyll's noblemen clamoured for her execution for infanticide and cannibalism. But her husband demurred, condemning her instead to the curious punishment of being made to greet visitors to *Llys Arberth* at the horse-block by the gate and to offer to carry them on her back to the court entrance. Bearing in mind Rhiannon's first appearance to Pwyll in their story, this was perhaps not so odd because it served to reinforce Rhiannon's essential connection to horses. This is a link that is followed up further as the tale unfolds, for the missing baby was not dead but later turned up mysteriously at the home of someone who bred champion horses.

The scene of the story then moves from Arberth to a place called Gwent-Is Coed (probably the region now known as the Gwent Levels, in south-east Wales) and a land ruled by a man called Teyrnon, described as the best man in the world, who owned the most wonderful mare in his kingdom. Teyrnon had a problem. His mare produced a foal each year on May Eve but every colt disappeared the moment it was born. This was the same day that Rhiannon's newborn baby had disappeared. Teyrnon decided to keep watch over his pregnant mare and, sure enough, as soon as the foal was born, a huge, scaly and clawed arm lunged through the stable window to grab the colt by its mane. Teyrnon drew his sword and struck off the arm. As he did so, he heard a great hullabaloo and a scream from outside. He rushed out but could see nothing because the night was so dark. When he returned to the stable, he was astonished to find a baby boy wrapped in a silken sheet, a sign of the child's noble birth.

Teyrnon and his wife decided to keep the baby and bring him up as their own. And he grew into a fine boy. He was very advanced for his age, so much so that when he was four years old he was big enough to take his foster-father's horses down to the river to drink. The child was so horse-mad that his foster-parents gave him the colt that had been saved on the day he had arrived. Meanwhile, gossip had reached and was circulating in Gwent-Is Coed concerning Arberth's lost baby and Rhiannon's punishment. Teyrnon and his wife realised that their foster-child looked exactly like Pwyll. They pondered what to do and decided that they should return the child to his true parents. Upon his return, there was rejoicing and feasting. Rhiannon's relief and joy were unbounded, and the boy was named Pryderi – a word meaning 'care' – his full name being Pryderi, son of Pwyll, Lord of Annwfn (Arawn had made Pwyll a lord of his realm as a reward for defeating Hafgan). Teyrnon and his wife were amply rewarded by Pwyll and Rhiannon. And, of course, the supernatural link between Pryderi and horses had been inherited from his mother who, herself, was perhaps perceived to have otherworldly origins.

Blessed and benighted: Brân and Branwen

The Second Branch of the *Mabinogion* is set far away from Arberth, at Harlech in Gwynedd. It concerns Brân the Blessed (otherwise known as Bendigeidfran), scion of the royal house of Llŷr, and his sister Branwen. Brân was cited as being king of the whole island of Britain, and was crowned in London. That he was of superhuman origin is evident in the manner in which he is described throughout the tale. For instance, he was too large to fit into any house and he could form bridges over rivers for his men to walk across. Apart from his sister, this godlike king had three brothers: Manawydan (whom we meet later, in the Third Branch), Nisien and Efnisien. (These last two figures are important for Nisien represented goodness and peace, while Efnisien was his brother's opposite – the bad twin – an inciter of friction and unrest and a bringer of calamity.)

The story begins with the sighting of thirteen ships approaching the north Welsh shore from Ireland. All the vessels were highly decorated, signifying their importance. Indeed, one of them carried Matholwch, the Irish king. The purpose of his journey to Harlech was to ask Brân for the hand of his sister and thus to cement the alliance between Wales and Ireland. Brân joyfully agreed (although Branwen was not consulted about the marriage) and the two were betrothed. The storyteller describes Branwen, in somewhat contradictory terms, as 'one of the three Matriarchs of the Island of Britain, as well as the fairest maiden [usually this term was equated with virginity] in the land'. I think this description was meant to flag up her credentials and, perhaps also, give hints to the audience that she might have been divine. The character of Branwen is interesting for she seems a pale, insubstantial player in the story, yet she would act as the catalyst for a hugely punishing and mutually destructive war between the two lands of Wales and Ireland.

All was set for the marriage, and the party travelled to Aberffraw (near the mouth of the Ffraw river, on Anglesey) for the nuptials and celebration feasts. But after the happy couple's first night together, the reckless Efnisien took centre stage. Feeling insulted because he was not consulted about his sister's betrothal to the Irish king, he set out to insult Matholwch by the most hideous and bizarre means. He crept into the stables under cover of darkness and mutilated all the Irish horses by cutting off their tails, lips, ears and eyelids so that they were fit for nothing. Matholwch was so angry when he heard this news that he packed up. He was ready to walk out, withdraw from the union (both from his marriage and the alliance between the two lands) and sail home. Brân begged him to reconsider, and offered him many precious gifts, but the Irish king refused them all. Then, he was offered something so valuable that even he could not resist the temptation to accept it: a magical cauldron of regeneration, capable of restoring the dead to life when they were dipped in the liquid contained inside. We will discover more about this cauldron and its origins in later chapters.

So, having accepted Brân's priceless gift, Matholwch set off for Ireland from Aber Menai, taking Branwen, his wife, with him. They were received with great joy by the king's people and, for a time at least, Branwen was a resounding success as his consort, acquiring a reputation for the lavishness of her generosity to anyone visiting the royal court. To everyone's delight, she soon became pregnant and gave birth to a son, whom they called Gwern. As was the custom of the time, the infant was put out to foster with the best family in the land for raising royal children. But, for some reason, in the second year of Matholwch and Branwen's marriage, people began to turn against the queen and started dredging up the insult to the king made by Efnisien, her brother. The spiteful murmuring against Branwen gained momentum, and she was banished to the kitchens as a slave, where she was beaten every day by the butcher. What is more, an embargo was put on all traffic between Ireland and Wales, meaning that Branwen had no means of contacting Brân for help.

Branwen was desperate. And it is here that the storyteller inserts an implication concerning her semi-divine status: she reared a starling and trained it (as a kind of early satnav) so that it could fly across to Harlech and seek out her brother, delivering her message in a letter tied to the bird's feet. It worked, and Brân promptly summoned his fighting-men and they sailed to Ireland for battle. Again, Brân's super-human nature is a part of the tale: he was so large that he waded across the Irish Sea and then later formed a bridge over a river with his body so that his army could march across him to the other side. The ensuing war was a bitter one. Ironically, Brân's gift to Matholwch was used by the Irish king against the Welsh: every one of his soldiers who died was resurrected in the cauldron of rebirth, so that the next day his forces fought better than ever. The only caveat was that the risen dead could no longer speak. They were zombies, not truly restored to human life, but still belonging to the realm of the dead.

Now Branwen and Brân's destructive brother, Efnisien, strides back onto the stage of our story. During peace talks between the opposing forces at Matholwch's court, he suddenly seized Gwern, Branwen and Matholwch's young son, and cast him into the fire in the hearth, where he burnt to death. In the end, this rogue character, Efnisien, redeemed himself by throwing himself into the fickle cauldron of rebirth,

---

A SEVERED HEAD
FROM ROMAN CAERWENT

In the fourth century AD, someone living in Caerwent, capital of the local Silurian tribe, carefully placed a life-size sculpture of a severed head in a private sanctum within the garden of a wealthy Roman house. The imagery of the mosaic floor of that house suggests that the owner was a Christian. The head, a powerful pagan symbol, may have been put in this makeshift shrine by someone who worked on the villa-owner's estate. The carving was deliberately designed as an image of a disembodied human head, rather than having been broken off of a statue. The face is arresting to look at, with round eyes and an open mouth, as if it is speaking. I have spent my career as an archaeologist (and myth-chaser) studying ancient cult images and I believe that this head represented an 'oracle stone', for it definitely appears to be speaking, like the Brân of Welsh legend.

stretching himself inside it so that it shattered, but bursting his heart in the process and therefore killing himself.

There were no winners in the war between Wales and Ireland as most fighters were killed. Brân was felled by a poisoned spear that pierced his foot (akin to the fate of the Greek mythic hero Achilles). As he was dying, he ordered his few surviving men to cut off his head and take it with them on their travels. He vowed that it would converse with them and continue to guide them for many years. And it does so until, at his command, they take it to London and bury it at the White Mount (perhaps the site of the Tower of London), facing France so that it can repel invaders. Branwen killed herself, full of sorrow that she had caused the fall of two great nations.

Manawydan, sorcery and empty lands

The story of Manawydan, Brân's other brother, is told in the Third Branch. Like his sibling, this man was wreathed around with magic: he possessed powers of wizardry. This Branch cleverly picks up threads from the First, putting Rhiannon and her son, Pryderi, centre stage alongside Manawydan. Pryderi was now grown-up and his father, Pwyll, had died. The young man not only invited Manawydan to leave Harlech but also offered him both his widowed mother in marriage and a large swathe of Dyfed as his fiefdom.

After the wedding feast at Arberth, Manawydan and his new bride, Rhiannon, went out hunting with Pryderi and his wife Cigfa. On their return, the four began feasting with their people. While everyone was partying, something cataclysmic happened: a deafening crack of thunder was followed by a totally enveloping mist. This event was triggered by a visit to the magic mound (the *Gorsedd*) made by the four protagonists during the celebrations. Pwyll's visit to the mound had resulted in his first sighting of Rhiannon but, on this occasion, the visit to the *Gorsedd* had a catastrophic outcome. When the mist lifted and bright light shone down, the two couples saw that all the other people, their dwellings and their domestic animals had disappeared. The land was empty for as far as they could see, except for the four of them, their horses and their hunting dogs. The court of Arberth itself still stood but it, too, was devoid of life.

After taking solace in more feasting and hunting, Manawydan and his three companions began to explore their surroundings, desperate to find anything in the deserted landscape. They managed to survive on fish and the flesh of hunted wild beasts. It is interesting that only farm animals had been affected by the vanishing spell. Perhaps this was because domestic beasts were the property of the people who had disappeared, while wild animals existed without any human involvement in their lives.

Despairing of their bleak life in Wales, Manawydan, Rhiannon, Pryderi and Cigfa turned eastwards and made for England. They took up residence in three towns, one after the other. The two men plied a different trade in each, all associated with Manawydan's magical skills. In Hereford, he and Pryderi made saddles. In the next town, they fashioned shields, and in the third they produced gilded shoes with the finest leather from Cordoba in Spain. Their products were the best in the land. But each time they exhibited their skills, they antagonised the local craftsmen, who drove them out with dire threats should they try to return. So at last, the wanderers turned west again. They returned to Wales where they lived by hunting again, for a time.

But now, more magic-driven misfortunes assailed the unhappy quartet. One day, while out hunting, they noticed their hounds backing away from a grove of trees, their hackles raised in fear. They investigated and found themselves confronted by an enormous wild boar. The creature was glistening white – like Rhiannon's shining white horse and Arawn's white dogs – letting the storyteller's audience know that all these beasts emanated from the otherworld.

The huge white boar lured the hunting dogs away from Manawydan and his companions, leading them towards a castle 'all newly built, in a place where they had never seen either stone or building'. But, once inside, all trace of the dogs vanished: no sight of them or sound of their barking. Against the advice of the others, Pryderi set out to explore the castle and find the dogs. When he entered, he could see neither human nor beast but only a golden bowl. When he reached out and touched it,

SACRED BOARS IN THE IRON AGE AND ROMAN BRITAIN AND GAUL

Iron Age coins and figurines repeatedly depict images of wild boars, always with their dorsal bristles erect, in fighting mode. One recent coin discovery depicts a human head wearing a boarskin hat with distinctively outlined bristles, as if the head is someone in boar-costume. It is interesting that the Gauls and Britons had great war-trumpets, called *carnyces* (singular *carnyx*), the mouthpieces of which were fashioned into boars' heads that could imitate both throaty and intimidating roars and also the squeaky noises of a piglet. Classical writers on the subject commented that massed *carnyces* were more frightening to enemies than swords and spears. An Iron Age shield found in the river Witham in Lincolnshire was decorated with a striking image of a boar in profile, with elongated legs and an exaggerated snout. There was even a Gallo-Roman boar-goddess called Arduinna, after the Ardennes Forest in which she was venerated. She is depicted in a small bronze figurine, riding a large-tusked boar with a short sword or knife in her right hand. Perhaps she represented a dichotomous deity who protected both wild boars and their hunters.

he found he was stuck fast: he could neither move his feet nor speak. His mother, Rhiannon, found him there and she too became imprisoned by its magical powers. Soon afterwards, there was another great thunderclap and another enveloping mist appeared. After the mist cleared once more, the castle and its two luckless occupants had disappeared.

Manawydan and Cigfa were all that was left of the quartet that had started out on this fateful hunting expedition. They retraced their steps to England and, once again, Manawydan plied his crafts and, once again, he and Cigfa were driven out by jealous traders. So the pair rode back to Dyfed where Manawydan acquired some wheat and planned to make a living by farming. The wheat was sown and it flourished – it was the finest wheat in the world, so the storyteller said. Soon the corn was ripe in one of the fields but, just before it was harvested, something (or some things) came and stripped the field bare. This happened in the second field, too, so Manawydan decided to keep watch over the third crop during the night before harvest. Lo and behold, an army of mice appeared and began devouring the ripe wheat. Manawydan gave chase, but the mice were faster. They scampered away, bearing the ears of corn with them, all but for one mouse, slower than the rest because she was pregnant. Manawydan caught her and his anger was so great that he put a noose round her neck and prepared to hang her, at the *Gorsedd Arberth*.

Just as he was rigging up the scaffold, a priest on horseback approached. He gave Manawydan and Cigfa God's blessing and enquired what they were doing. Manawydan told him, and the priest offered him bounty for the pregnant mouse's release. He was refused. Then a bishop came and he also tried, and failed, to get Manawydan to stay his hand, offering him many rich gifts. The holy man confessed that it was he who had brought about the enchantments on Dyfed, and that the mice were humans changed into animals by his own magic. It is interesting that a Christian clergyman could also be a wizard. When the bishop asked him to name his price for the mouse's freedom, Manawydan said that he would think about letting the mouse go if the bishop lifted the spell he had put on the castle, and set Pryderi and Rhiannon free.

It turned out that that the hapless pregnant mouse, about to be hanged, was the bishop-sorcerer's shape-changed wife. He explained that he had effected this magic in order to settle an old score, referring to the marriage between Pwyll and Rhiannon after Pwyll had tricked his rival suitor, Gwawl, to win Rhiannon's hand. All ended well: Dyfed was restored, the convicted mouse was changed back into 'the fairest young woman that anyone had seen' and the sticking-spell fell away from Pryderi and Rhiannon. Interestingly, when Manawydan asked what punishment the bishop-sorcerer had conjured for the enchanted pair, he announced that both of them were haltered and used, like horses, to carry hay. And so the horse symbolism surrounding Rhiannon and her son in the First Branch was fleetingly revisited in the Third Branch. The mention of Manawydan's wheat-growing in his story is also significant, for it may contain a mythic explanation for the beginning of farming in Wales. In the Fourth Branch, the farming reference emerges again, with a reference to animal husbandry in the keeping of pigs.

Magic and mayhem: the kingdom of Math

The scene in the Fourth Branch switches from Dyfed back to Gwynedd, a kingdom ruled by Math, a monarch skilled in magic. Immediately, we are made aware of something rather peculiar about Math: unless he was away at war, he could not survive unless his feet were cradled in a virgin's lap. Interestingly, historical sources – as opposed to myths – make allusion to royal foot-holders, but such courtiers were always male. In this case the foot-holders are women and the virginity angle is introduced, I think, to set the stage for the tale, because female chastity (and its absence) crops up again as an essential element later on.

Math had two nephews, brothers named Gwydion and Gilfaethwy. Like his uncle, Gwydion possessed magical powers (which would ultimately lead to mischief and misfortune). Gilfaethwy lusted after Math's foot-holder. Her name was Goewin. In order to get access to her, the brothers contrived to get Math out of the way by fomenting conflict between Gwynedd and Dyfed. Gwydion whispered in Math's ear that the southern kingdom had wonderful animals – pigs whose flesh was much sweeter than beef. These animals had been gifts to Pwyll of Dyfed from Arawn, lord of Annwfn (the otherworld) in gratitude for Pwyll's help in defeating his rival Hafgan. So Gwydion went south and stole the herd of pigs, thus bringing about war between Pryderi's kingdom and Math's. This, of course, meant that the King of Gwynedd had to leave his home – and Goewin – to fight, leaving the way open for Gilfaethwy to have his wicked way with her. The war between Dyfed and Gwynedd ended with single combat between Pryderi and Gwydion: the latter used his magic to kill his opponent.

When Math returned and discovered the truth, his anger knew no bounds. In vengeance for his nephews' perfidy and the defilement of Goewin, he deployed his magician's powers against them. The spells cast upon them as punishment are interesting. Math turned them both into gendered pairs of animals: a stag and hind for a year, a boar and sow for the second year, and a wolf and she-wolf for the third. At the end of each year, the pair produced offspring in animal form. But the spell was even more intricate because the genders were swapped around, so that Gilfaethwy shape-changed into a hind and Gwydion a stag, then Gilfaethwy became a boar and Gwydion a sow, and so on. After three years, Math then turned the offspring into comely, strong boys, each named for the animal-form into which he had been born. He also turned his treacherous nephews back to their true selves.

And now Math had the urgent task of replacing Goewin as his virgin foot-holder. (By the way, he married her, now she was despoiled, at least according to the standards of the time.) Gwydion came forward with a suggestion: that Math should choose his own niece, Aranrhod, for the role. This is our introduction to a new player on the stage. As the story of Math nears its close, Aranrhod takes the central position. Math didn't wish to be duped again so he set the applicant a test. He placed his magic wand on the ground and commanded her to step over it, to prove her maidenhood. Alas, Aranrhod failed the test abysmally, giving birth to two fine boys as she put her foot over the wand.

One of her children, Dylan, escaped into the sea as soon as he was born, but was later slain by Gofannon, his uncle. The other child was cursed by Aranrhod, presumably because of the shame his birth had brought on her. She laid three curses upon the luckless boy: that he would have no name unless she named him; that he would never bear arms unless she armed him; and, finally, that he would never marry.

Gwydion was greatly grieved by these spells. He scooped up the second baby, before anyone saw him, and hid him in a chest. He loved him as the boy grew up to be big and strong and, like Pryderi as a child, he was precocious in both stature and understanding. So, using his own powers of magic, he managed to trick Aranrhod into giving the boy a name – Lleu Llaw Gyffes (meaning 'fair' and 'deft-handed'), and arming him, but he was stuck when it came to finding a bride for the youth. What could he do?

The two magicians, Math and Gwydion, put their heads together to sort out a wife for Lleu. They came up with the idea of creating a woman out of flowers. They took blooms from the oak, meadowsweet and broom, and from all the wild plants that each flowered at a different time of the year. With these blooms, they fashioned something that looked and be-haved like a woman, naming her Blodeuwedd ('Flower Face'). The two were married but, because Blodeuwedd was not truly human, she had no human morality. (I suspect that the Christian ethic was at work in this part of the story.) And so she was unfaithful to Lleu, and took a lover, Gronw. The guilty pair conspired to get rid of Lleu for good, but there was a problem: because of his uncle Gwydion's protective magic, he was virtually immortal. However, they knew that there was a complicated and secret way round this impasse. Blodeuwedd exerted all her feminine wiles on her unsuspecting and, frankly, somewhat dim-witted husband. In honeyed tones, she asked him how his death could be brought about. And he took the bait, hook, line and sinker.

Gronw dealt the vulnerable Lleu a killing blow with a poisoned spear, but then magic supervened once more: instead of collapsing dead on the ground, the mortally wounded Lleu morphed into a great eagle and, giving a wild screech, flew to shelter in a giant oak tree. It was there that Gwydion eventually found him, tracking him down with the aid of a swineherd, who had reported to him that his prize sow vanished each day and could not be found until she returned. So Gwydion lay in wait for her to burst out of her sty one morning and followed her to Lleu's oak, where he discovered her feeding on some flesh at its base. Gwydion looked up, saw the eagle and recognised his transformed nephew. He was a sorry sight to behold, worm-ridden, with great lumps of rotting flesh showering from him when he shook himself. Gwydion sang him a special poem, called an *englyn*, to entice him down. And the great bird perched on his knee as the magician touched him with his magic wand, turning him back into a man. Like Lazarus, raised from the dead by Jesus in the New Testament, he was never the same again, though.

Now it was time for revenge for the wrongs done to Lleu. First, Gwydion turned to the faithless Blodeuwedd. She wasn't killed but instead turned into an owl, destined to be shunned by all other birds and to live a solitary life, hunting by night, and never to see daylight again. It was Lleu himself who punished Gronw, breaking his back with the very spear he had been attacked with, in a fitting end. So Lleu was avenged.

The Fourth Branch is even more steeped in magic than the other three. Magicians stalk through the myth, and their magical deeds abound. And shape-changing between humans and animals is even more prominent here than heretofore. In my view, this Branch is the richest, most complex, multi-layered and supernaturally charged of the four. Once again there is a skilful reference to themes within the other tales. A prime example is Arawn's supernatural pigs, clearly with connections to the otherworld, that unwittingly lead to the great war between Dyfed and Gwynedd. In a manner similar to Manawydan's wheat-growing in the Third Branch, this myth attempts to explain the origin of pig-farming in Wales.

Star-crossed lovers: the story of Culhwch and Olwen

This mythic tale is separate from the Four Branches but it belongs to the wider group of eleven stories under the loose umbrella of the *Mabinogion*. It is full of enchantments, weird beings – such as savage giants and shape-shifting creatures – and pigs, again, play a large part in the narrative. The central character is Culhwch, whose name means 'pig-run'. His father was a king, named Cilydd and his queen's name was Goleuddydd. The boy got his strange name thus: when his mother was about to give birth to him, she wandered past a herd of pigs and was so terrified by the sight of them that she immediately went into labour, and so the baby was born in a pig-run. His mother died and, after a period of mourning, his father sought a new wife. His counsellors found one for him but she was already married, so

LLEU AS A GOD OF LIGHT

One of the principal gods of the Gallo-British pantheon of
the first to the fourth centuries AD (with his origins possibly even earlier, in later prehistory) was a solar-sky god,
affiliated to the Roman Jupiter but with his own individual
symbolism. The many images of him, carved in stone and
hoisted high on great stone pillars, depict him on horseback,
fighting an underworld monster. His shield is sometimes in
the form of a solar wheel. Iron Age gold coins frequently
display horses beneath huge wheel-shaped sun-symbols.
What is more, the pillars themselves are often in the form
of tree trunks, decorated with oak leaves. These 'Jupiter-
Giant' columns were erected in the Rhineland, in Gaul and
in Britannia. The nearest to Wales so far discovered was in
Cirencester in the Cotswolds. Jupiter himself was a thun-
der-god, his celestial attributes including thunderbolts and
eagles. He was sometimes known by a Gallo-British name
'Taranis', cognate with the Welsh word for thunder, 'taran'.
And this god is named on a Romano-British altar erected at
Chester, near the Welsh border.

Lleu's association with eagles and oak trees links him to
Jupiter, and I wonder whether, in some way, his character
was influenced by the earlier divine footprint of the Roman
god. Images of Jupiter might well have still stood during the
time of the sacred journeys made by the monks who acted
as scribes for these stories that percolated down to medieval
times when they were first immortalised in writing.

Lleu's name means 'light'. Interestingly, light is also referenced in the name of his mother, Aranrhod, whose name
means 'silver wheel' (probably relating to the moon). And
one of the many links between Welsh and Irish mythology

manifests itself in that, like Lleu, the Irish god Lugh was also a god of light. Incidentally, Lugh's name turns up in ancient British and Gallic place names, such as Lugovalium (Carlisle) and Lugdunum (Lyon).

Cilydd's counsellors murdered her husband and brought the widow and her daughter to their king's court. As the boy grew, his stepmother began to plan a marriage between him and her daughter. But Culhwch demurred and – furious at the spurning of her child – the queen used magic to curse him, telling him that he would never find a wife until he found and successfully courted a girl named Olwen whose father, Ysbaddaden Bencawr (Chief Giant), was known for his ferocity against would-be suitors of his daughter.

Culhwch fell under his stepmother's spell and, although he had never set eyes on Olwen, he fell deeply and obsessively in love with her, and determined to win her hand. His father, Cilydd, advised that he should go to the court of King Arthur, Culhwch's cousin, and ask him to trim his hair. It may seem a strange thing to suggest but I suspect that it references an ancient kinship ritual where the cutting of hair or shaving by someone else represented blood-ties, affiliation and support. So the boy went to Arthur's court. At first, he was denied access by the gatekeeper because he was unannounced. In his rage, Culhwch threatened to shriek so loudly that all pregnant women at the court would miscarry (this was perhaps a storytelling device to display Culhwch's divine status to the audience). And so, he was admitted to Arthur's court where he asked for the favour. Arthur willingly took the comb and shears and cut his hair. As he performed this task, Arthur realised that Culhwch was his kin and told the youth to ask any favour he wished. Culhwch replied that he wanted the help of Arthur and his retinue in finding Olwen so that he could marry her.

The story continues to unfold with the summoning of a multitude of Arthur's warriors, including some we have already met, such as Manawydan. Many of these men possessed superhuman powers. For instance, Cei could hold his breath under water for nine days and nights and go without sleep for nine nights. He could also grow very tall as and when he wished, and his sword could inflict wounds that no doctor could heal. Another knight, Gwrhyr, could speak any language, including the language of animals. That power was to prove very useful in Culhwch's quest for Olwen.

After much searching, the quest to find Olwen was successful. The author of the story describes her in great detail, hinting that she was someone very special. She was clothed in red silk, wearing a great gold and gem-studded torc (necklet). She had the yellowest of hair, the whitest of skin, and the reddest of cheeks. In short, she was devastatingly beautiful. Culhwch approached and told her of his passion for her. She requited his love but explained to him that there was one big problem: her father, the giant Ysbaddaden. This monster was so enormous that he needed the aid of two forks to raise his eyelids. He was bitterly opposed to his daughter's marriage because he had an injunction (like a spell) placed upon him that he could only remain alive while Olwen was single. So he told Culhwch that Olwen could only be his wife if the boy fulfilled a set of virtually impossible tasks (rather in the manner of the Labours of Heracles in Greek mythology). One of the tasks was to bring to him the three singing birds of Rhiannon, which had the power to wake the dead as well as lull the living to sleep. But the greatest tasks of all those that Ysbaddaden laid on Culhwch were all regarding the giant's hair. He demanded blood from the Black Witch to calm his recalcitrant beard and – the most perilous of all the tasks – that he be brought the comb, razor and shears that nestled in the bristles of a huge, enchanted boar, named Twrch Trwyth.

So the quest for the great boar began. In order to hunt him successfully, Culhwch needed to obtain an especially powerful hunting dog, called Drudwyn. This was an animal that could only be tamed by using a magical leash and collar and, what is more, the hound would only work with a divine huntsman. This huntsman was Mabon, son of Modron, and tracking him down proved to be the most daunting of the many 'impossible tasks' heaped upon Culhwch and Arthur. The quest for Mabon proved so difficult that Arthur's man Gwrhyr was deployed to speak to any animals that might help. He spoke to a blackbird, a stag, an owl, an eagle (described as the oldest in the world), and the Salmon of Llyn Llyw, who was the wisest and most helpful of all the animals. The Salmon of Llyn Llyw was a gigantic fish, and Cei and Gwrhyr were able to ride the river on his back until they came to the fortress of Caer Loyw in Gloucester. There, they heard someone lamenting: it was Mabon,

MABON AND MAPONUS

There is an exciting linguistic connection between Mabon, the great hunter that helped Culhwch bring down Twrch Trwyth, and the much earlier Romano-British deity Maponus. Both names mean 'young son' or 'divine youth'. Like Mabon, Maponus was a hunter-god, sometimes equated with the Roman god Apollo as he shared other characteristics with him, including a role as a god of light and of music. During excavations at the Roman fort of Vindolanda (now Chesterholm), just south of Hadrian's Wall, a unique silver crescent-shaped plaque dedicated to Maponus was discovered. Perhaps this small object was a personal keepsake belonging to a worshipper or maybe it was a gift to the god – an offering once placed on the altar of a forgotten shrine as a votive or perhaps asking or thanking Maponus for some favour. These links between a Romano-British deity and a Welsh medieval mythic figure suggest that some religious memories survived for hundreds of years after the Roman occupation of Britannia and infiltrated some of the Welsh mythic stories, both in oral and later written traditions.

imprisoned in the castle. Arthur's warriors stormed the fortress and rescued Mabon, so he was free to help in the quest for Twrch Trwyth.

It wasn't going to be easy to hunt down the great boar. The pursuit took them to Ireland, Cornwall, Devon, Brittany and southern Wales. The giant animal roamed with several porcine companions, and it transpired that all of the boars had once been men but had been transformed into swine by God (the Christian God) because of their wicked deeds. Twrch Trwyth had been a king. At last, after much bloodshed, Twrch Trwyth was cornered, and robbed of his grooming articles. Culhwch and Olwen married and remained together for life. But her father, Ysbaddaden, met a grisly end. Culhwch ordered his companion, Gorau, to cut the giant's head off and stick it on a post for all to see. It is interesting that the tale of Culhwch's quest for Olwen begins and ends with the common theme of pigs. He was born near a domestic pigsty and named for his birthplace, and his destiny lay in the conquest of a huge, wild and supernaturally-enchanted boar.

'The Tale of Taliesin'

According to some scholars, this tale dates considerably later than the stories in the *Mabinogion*, and perhaps should be seen as a folktale rather than a myth. I disagree because it contains such resonances with other Welsh mythic themes. In its earliest surviving written form it dates to the Tudor period, around 1550. But it is redolent with the supernatural and contains many facets that indicate strong links with earlier narratives. One of the stories in 'The Tale of Taliesin' is particularly significant: the story of Ceridwen's cauldron. We have already encountered the cauldron of rebirth that played such a pivotal role in the Second Branch of the *Mabinogi*. Ceridwen may be described as a debased goddess or a witch with magical powers. She had two sons: one called Crearwy (meaning 'light' or 'beautiful one') and the other, an ugly, surly youth, was called Afagddu (meaning 'total darkness'), and she despised him. But Ceridwen decided to make up for Afagddu's misfortunes by boiling up a stew for him in her cauldron which, when he tasted it, would make him wise and all-knowing. However, his mother gave a little boy, Gwion, the responsibility of tending the fire heating the cauldron while she slept. When its contents boiled over, three drops of the magical stew spat out and landed on the child's thumb. Instinctively, Gwion stuck his scalded thumb in his mouth and, thereby, unwittingly stole Afagddu's inheritance. Realising how angry Ceridwen would be at his accidental treachery in snatching the power meant for Afagddu, Gwion fled the scene. Ceridwen immediately gave chase, but his newfound powers enabled the fleeing boy to evade the witch by turning himself into a hare. In response, she shape-shifted to a greyhound. Then the pair changed again: he to a river-fish and she to an otter; and finally, he to a bird and she to a hawk. The final change saw Gwion turning into a grain of wheat and Ceridwen to a hen. Inevitably, she ate him but, after nine months, Gwion was reborn as a sumptuously beautiful child whom his 'mother' could not bear to kill. Instead, mirroring what happened to Moses in his basket in the Old Testament of the Bible, Ceridwen put him into a coracle and it floated away on the sea. A fisherman rescued him and called the child Taliesin, meaning 'shining face', because of his radiance. On account of his shape-shifting abilities, Taliesin became best known as a shaman. In many traditional societies, shamans were recognised for their power to turn themselves into animals, usually in order to cross the portal between the human and spirit worlds. We will learn more about shamans later on in this book.

Conclusion

In this first chapter, we've mapped out a pathway through the labyrinth of Welsh mythology. By no means all relevant mythic stories have been included here, but particular themes within those omitted will be picked up in the chapters that follow, where we will flesh out and explore important specific features of the narratives. In the pages that follow, we'll discover the richness of Welsh mythic literature, which bursts with otherworldly happenings, superhuman beings (whether shiningly good or creepily evil), and peculiar objects with special powers that can work with, or against, humans. Let the games begin!

Brân continues to speak to his companions,
after they follow his request to sever his head from his body.

CHAPTER 2

Gods and Heroes

Bendigeidfran came to land and a fleet with him, towards the bank of the river. 'Lord,' said his noblemen, 'thou knowest the peculiarity of the river: none can go through it, nor is there a bridge over it. What is thy counsel as to a bridge?' said they. 'There is none,' said he, 'save that he who is chief, let him be a bridge. I will myself be a bridge,' said he ... And then, after he had lain him down across the river, hurdles were placed upon him, and his hosts passed through over him.

Hidden gods?

Brân (Bendigeidfran) is a prime example of the otherworldly nature of many of the principal characters in the Welsh myths. References to his godlike status pepper his narrative. He was of prodigious size. His chronicler describes how, when a feast was planned in his honour by the Irish king Matholwch, he had to have a special 'tent' constructed to contain him for he was too large to fit into any normal dwelling. He was even big enough to wade across the Irish Sea from Wales to Ireland. Brân met a strange end: in the final episode of the Second Branch, when dealt a mortal wound, he commanded his men to cut off his head and to take it with them, promising that it would remain 'alive' and guide them on their subsequent travels.

Superhuman powers inevitably surrounded the principal characters of the mythic tales, and these were used for either good or evil. But were these characters really watered-down or veiled deities, or simply creatures conjured up by storytellers to charge up their stories with the excitement of the paranormal? Although certain connections between Irish and Welsh myths may be identified, Irish mythology is different. The Irish stories were written down centuries before the Welsh ones and, in the former, the pagan gods that are featured are treated and acknowledged as such. So, for example, in the '*Táin Bó Cuailnge*' ('The Cattle Raid of Cooley'), distinctions are made between the hero Cú Chulainn and the battle-goddess known as the Morrigán. She was a deity and, though he certainly had heroic qualities, he was not.

There are some interesting divine connections between the myths of Ireland and Wales. The Irish god of light, Lugh, is almost certainly cognate with the hapless Lleu in the Fourth Branch. Lleu's celestial link is indicated by his transformation into an eagle. And the Irish metalsmith-god, Goibhniu, is likely to have had his Welsh counterpart in the undeveloped character Gofannon, son of Dôn (head of the divine dynasty of Gwynedd), who appears in the Fourth Branch (as the killer of Aranrhod's firstborn son, Dylan) and in the tale of 'Culhwch and Olwen'. Dôn herself is the Welsh counterpart of the Irish mother-goddess Danu. And, of course, there are the obvious links between the two countries themselves in the Second Branch and the story of the doomed marriage between Branwen and Matholwch.

It remains, though, that the interesting, and perhaps date-driven, difference between the superhuman beings that inhabit the myths of Wales and Ireland is that the Welsh characters are not overtly displayed as deities, while the pagan pantheon of Ireland is blatantly expressed as such. It seems as though, in Welsh mythic tradition, the beings that had once been gods within a pagan pantheon had been demoted and were treated not as divine but as heroes. Some, like Brân, possess certain elements of immortality – evidenced by his severed head still talking after its owner's decapitation. For the most part, though, these arch-beings succumbed to the same ends as mortal people. And, unlike the Irish narratives, God – the Christian God – is mentioned in many of the Welsh stories, although Christianity itself is never explored in any detail.

In Welsh mythology, the Christian God was intimately associated with good morals and ethical behaviour. For instance, in the story of 'Culhwch and Olwen', we are told that the evil deeds done by Twrch Trwyth and his fellow travellers were punished by God when they were turned into boars. But when Culhwch and Arthur set out on their almost impossible quest to find the magical boar, they did not call upon the Christian God for help but rather relied on the skills of Arthur's men, supernaturally endowed animals and – if we are to acknowledge the link between Mabon, the supreme hunter of the story, and the Romano-British god Maponus – on beings that were the remnants of the old pagan system.

The role of the hero

In the first chapter, we were introduced to beings that were physically gigantic, like Brân, or endowed with superhuman qualities, like Manawydan or Rhiannon. They stalk the pages of the written tales and, by inference, they were present in the oral stories that preceded them. All of the big players on this multifarious stage are described as breaking the normal bonds of humanity and as having particular gifts and skills that raised them above mere people. Even Branwen, perhaps sometimes perceived as a bit of a milksop and dominated by her menfolk, has a supernatural edge: hence her ability to train a starling to understand human speech so that it could track down her brother following her mistreatment at the hands of her adopted Irish kin.

So, if the theory that the heroes (male or female) of the Welsh stories are watered-down or demoted deities is valid, then obvious care has been taken by the storytellers to project divine characteristics onto these larger-than-life beings. Some of them, like Rhiannon and Arawn, have close links with the otherworld – the realm of the spirits and the dead. As lord (or one of them) of the otherworld, Arawn seems very close to being a god himself, yet he could not overcome his rival, Hafgan, by means of his own powers and needed a flesh-and-blood human, Pwyll, to fight his battles for him. So there is an ambivalence, perhaps even a deliberate discord, between apparently powerful beings that belong to the world of the dead, and their weakness in comparison with living people.

This flaw in Arawn's power is interesting, in terms of how the otherworld was perceived. You may recall that Brân, Lord of Harlech, possessed a cauldron, greatly prized because of its capacity to offer rebirth to the dead whose bodies were dunked in the water inside. But this vessel of regeneration was not entirely what it seemed. Certainly, warriors slain in battle were 'reborn', so much so that they could return to fight the enemy even more proficiently than before. But, despite their renewed 'life', something was missing: they no longer had the power of speech. So, in a sense, they were 'undead': capable of performing most physical actions but lacking one of their key powers. This is important because – particularly for a storyteller – having a voice was so key. Bear in mind that, before literacy was endemic, speaking was virtually the only means of communication, of passing on information and knowledge, and of making connections between past and present. For oral narrators, if you couldn't speak, you were not truly alive. And this brings us back to Arawn. Powerful as he was in his reign over the world of the afterlife, he lacked certain essential capacities in his otherworld kingdom. So Pwyll, the living Overlord of Dyfed, was called upon to carry out a task that Arawn could not. Conversely, in a subtle inversion of that story, even when Brân had been decapitated, his severed head *was* capable of speaking to his followers, signalling to the audience that this mighty hero was so powerful that even his death could not rob him of his capacity to guide, advise and comfort his people.

Heroic magic in the First Branch

It is important to stress that Pwyll, Lord of Dyfed, and his son Pryderi were mortal: their deaths are chronicled in the mythic tales. The difference between gods and heroes was immortality: gods lived forever but heroes did not, despite their superhuman status and their links with the divine. (In Greek mythology, despite being the son of the goddess Thetis, Achilles was mortal.) The tale of Pwyll and Rhiannon contains many magical happenings. Yet, when the first scene opens, Pwyll's meeting with Arawn, lord of Annwfn, is related as if it was not a particularly special event. Likewise, the otherworld itself, home of spirits and the

SPEECHLESS HEADS

Images of decapitated heads were common to Britain and parts of Europe during the Iron Age and Roman periods. In the Lower Rhône Valley area of southern France, a number of stone temples (circa sixth–third century BC) displayed stone heads, sometimes, as at Entremont, depicted in groups. Some of the heads were carved without lips. There is one particularly striking sculpture from this site, a tall pillar that once stood upright but was later pulled down and placed flat as a threshold stone. Several outlines of human heads decorate this column and, when the stone was in its original position, all of them faced outwards and forward towards the viewer, eye to eye – except one. The head at the bottom of the carving was placed upside down, as if heading for the underworld. And all twelve of them were depicted mouthless.

Of course, it would be crass to assume direct links between a temple in southern France erected in the later first millennium BC and Welsh mythic narratives first written down in the medieval period. However, I do wonder whether early carvings similar to this might have still been visible in the landscapes seen by early Christian travelling pilgrims from Ireland or Wales. These carvings might, just might, have inspired oral traditions, and so found a place in tales such as the story of Brân. I am irresistibly reminded of the severed stone head found at Caerwent. Far from speechless, its open mouth resonates with the idea of the Welsh hero's head, that continued to talk even after it was parted from his body.

ancestral dead, is portrayed as if its boundaries are easily crossed. Pwyll's sojourn in Annwfn resonates strongly, for me at least, both with the early Irish hero Cú Chulainn's sojourn in the otherworld, and with the Trojan hero Aeneas's journey to Avernus, the underworld of Greek myth. The dark worlds of the dead were perceived as prohibited for the living, because intercourse between the material and spirit realms was deemed disruptive to the balance of both: leaving a gap in one and a surfeit of beings in the other. Both Cú Chulainn and Aeneas were warned – the Irish hero by the goddess of war and death, the Morrigán, and Aeneas by Apollo's oracle, the Sybil of Cumae – that descent to the underworld was easy but dangerous and that they might never be able to return to the land of the living. Pwyll's bargain with Arawn was agreed after Pwyll's act of cheating during a hunt, and so he was honour-bound to obey Arawn's injunction to stay in Annwfn for a year and to fight for the otherworld lord's kingdom. And, as we saw in the previous chapter, Pwyll took his honour and loyalty to Arawn to another level, in refraining from sleeping with the other king's wife while he dwelt in Annwfn.

The audience, listening to the stories in the First Branch, would be aware that something momentous was about to happen before it occurred because, as is true for modern soap operas, the storytellers would lay down anticipatory clues in order to keep their listeners enthralled. And this is amply reflected in Pwyll's first encounter with Rhiannon, who was to become his wife and the mother of his son. The magical mound, or *Gorsedd*, upon which he sat when he caught his first glimpse of her, must surely have represented the gateway to the otherworld, where unearthly things took place. The audience would have guessed this, tensing themselves for the wonders to come. And maybe the tale-teller would take the opportunity, at this juncture, to break off until the next episode. Rhiannon's appearance was ethereal and wreathed about with light: her horse gleamed snowy-white and she herself was clad in brocaded gold cloth. Here, the storyteller would indulge in elaborate word-painting, in order to make hearers 'see' the vibrant colours being described. But what gave Rhiannon's other-worldliness away, above all, was the apparent contradiction implied by her mount's speed: while it never seemed to gallop fast, human riders could never catch up with it. Gateways and thresholds are common themes in myths and they are often especially charged with power and magic. Pwyll's *Gorsedd* was one such boundary place.

The story of Pwyll's and Rhiannon's marriage is shot through with magic. Rhiannon's wedding to Pwyll was a happy event, and for a time she flourished, and became known for her generosity to her own people and to strangers. All seemed to go well until Pwyll's court began to murmur restively at her apparent barrenness. It was three years before she finally conceived. The number three has an importance in Welsh mythology which we shall explore in a later chapter and it clearly held especial significance here. Everyone rejoiced when she bore Pwyll a male heir until the baby went missing on his first night. Significantly, the child had been born on May Eve, which was a particularly important and supernatural date. This date marked the marginal, threshold time at the beginning of summer. The storyteller's audience would have been aware of such seasonal festivals and we can imagine the intake of breath in expectation of peculiar happenings at this edgy time.

We know more about these pagan festivals from Irish medieval texts. Each of the four seasons was celebrated with particular sacred rites. Beltane was the name of the early May ceremony in Irish mythology, when druids would drive herds of cattle between twin bonfires, in ritual purification acts. In both Irish and Welsh mythic traditions, it appears that all these 'boundary' events were heavily ritualised because they were freighted with danger. For instance, the Irish New Year festival of Samhain (31 October–1 November, like our Hallowe'en and All Saints' Day), was regarded as a perilous time because the borders between the material and spirit worlds temporarily gaped open, meaning that the ghosts of the dead and the gods were free to roam and make mischief in the world of humans. Although less is known about these seasonal festivals in Welsh mythic narratives, the strange occurrences on May Eve in the First Branch of the *Mabinogion* make sense against such a backdrop of fear and danger. In terms of continuity between Romano-Gallic and medieval Welsh traditions, it is worth noting that Samhain was also celebrated in ancient Gaul. The great Gallo-Roman calendar discovered in Coligny in central France consists of a large sheet of bronze marked with writing that lists major festivals and religious days, of which one of the former was 'Samonios', a word linguistically linked with Samhain.

So Rhiannon was triply cursed: firstly in her initial failure to produce a child, secondly in the baby's disappearance as soon as it had been born, and thirdly in being framed for her son's murder (and consumption). Her punishment neatly reminded listeners of her strong bond with horses, drawing together the threads of Pwyll's first sighting of her on her magical horse with her shame at being treated like a beast of burden.

All was made well by the ending of the First Branch, but the narrator reminds us that, despite his supernatural encounters, Pwyll has died and is mortal. There is less clarity about Rhiannon's nature. Her story is picked up in the Third Branch, and Rhiannon's horse-symbolism, spelt out in the First Branch, is reinforced at the end of the Third, in the punishment meted out to her under the spell of wizardry. To add to all her other misfortunes brought about by sorcery, Rhiannon's heroic connection to horses was turned on its head, when she was yoked, like an ass, hauling hay, while imprisoned in the enchanted castle with her son.

Interestingly, in the Third Branch when her son Pryderi encouraged Manawydan to marry his widowed mother, he emphasised her worth by referring to her unsurpassed ability at conversation. Perhaps this 'jewel in her crown' was meant to reaffirm to audiences how important was the power of speech, and how its lack (for instance in the speech-less soldiers reborn in Brân's magic cauldron) denied humanity.

Rhiannon's connection with the otherworld is maintained in the Second Branch and the tale of 'Culhwch and Olwen', in the enigmatic references to the three 'singing birds of Rhiannon' which dwelt in Annwfn. In the Second Branch, these supernatural birds comforted Brân's companions on their journey with their chieftain's severed head. And in the tale of 'Culhwch and Olwen', one of Culhwch's 'impossible' tasks, laid on him by Olwen's father Ysbaddaden, was to seek out Rhiannon's singing birds.

Brân, Manawydan and Math

Like Pwyll and Rhiannon, the three heroes whose tales are told respectively in the Second, Third and Fourth Branches were each charged with superhuman powers. Manawydan and Math were overtly described as magicians, while Brân's superhuman status was reflected both in his prodigious size and in his severed head's ability to remain 'alive'. His power also lay with his most precious possession, the cauldron of rebirth, which, as we have seen (and will explore further later in the book) was capricious and able to turn on its owner and betray him.

All three have in common the contradiction of power and calamity. Brân was destroyed partly by the caprice of his cauldron and ultimately by the Irish king Matholwch's poisoned spear. Manawydan's kingdom disappeared after he and his kin visited the *Gorsedd* and his subsequent efforts to rebuild his world were thwarted by a vengeful rival magician, who vented his spleen on him and his companions by casting evil spells upon them. And, of course, despite his magical skills, Math's destiny was thwarted by his nephews' perfidy in robbing him of his virgin foot-holder. These curses are interesting, for they resonate both with Irish *gessa* (prohibitions) that occur repeatedly in Irish mythic stories, and with the curse tablets, written on lead or pewter sheets in the late Iron Age and Roman period contexts of Iberia, Gaul and Britannia.

Flawed heroes and anti-heroes

While larger-than-life persons, such as Brân, Math, Lleu and Rhiannon, are presented as being virtually without blemish to their character, others – like Gwydion – appear to be flawed, and some – like Efnisien and Blodeuwedd – definitely fall into the category of anti-hero.

All the great characters in the body of Welsh myth are projected as having strengths and weaknesses, to an extent. Rhiannon's problems (her baby son's disappearance, the false accusations against her, and her subsequent shameful punishments) can all be attributed to ill-luck or malign forces. But it may also be that the listener or reader would make a connection between her misfortunes and her presence in Dyfed despite her otherworldly origins. To put it bluntly, she didn't belong to the human world and paid the price for her encroachment therein. Lleu's troubles are founded in the blights brought upon him by women: Aranrhod, his mother, and his false wife, Blodeuwedd, the fake woman

THE CAERLEON CURSE

Cursing magic, set down in writing, is known to have been rife in ancient Britain and Gaul from at least the first century BC. Some of these curses (known as *defixiones* because they were designed to be 'fixed' on their intended victims) were incredibly savage and vindictive. On some of the curse tablets, they were referred to as *duscelinata* (evil death songs). These may actually have been chanted by ill-wishers, urging bad luck to rain down on their unfortunate victims, for whom simply the knowledge of the curse may have triggered a psychological blight that wrecked their lives. From Roman Britain, curse tablets have been discovered in quantities at the temples at Bath (Somerset) and Uley (Gloucestershire), and other scattered examples have been found elsewhere. One prominent *defixio* was excavated from the amphitheatre at the legionary fortress at Caerleon (Gwent). It reads thus:

'Lady Nemesis. I give thee a cloak and a pair of boots; let him who wore them not redeem them except with the life of his Blood-red charger.'

While this curse seeks to exact vengeance with the threat against the life of a horse, other *defixiones* were even more savage in their demands to the gods and frequently urged sacred powers to inflict hideous illnesses, infertility and death on their human targets. The choice of Nemesis as the divine avenger at Caerleon (in whose amphitheatre so much death occurred) is apt, for she was the goddess of fate and would be perceived to have particular power in the dangerous world of gladiatorial combat.

wrought from wild flowers by his uncle, Gwydion. He was the 'victim' of the Fourth Branch because of the curses laid upon him by his resentful mother. His quasi-divinity did not prevent him from being slain by his wife's lover, although – godlike – he was transformed and then resurrected by that same uncle. So, the story had a sort of fairy-tale-like 'happy ending', although Lleu remained scarred by his death and resurrection.

Prime examples of anti-heroes can be found in the presentation of Efnisien, in the Second Branch, and Gwydion, in the Fourth Branch. Efnisien and his brother Nisien were siblings of Brân but the story-teller emphasises that, unlike Branwen and Manawydan, who were the offspring of Llŷr, the supreme (and probably divine) chieftain of Harlech, these twins are 'two brothers on the mother's side'. It might be inferred from this that they were born 'the wrong side of the blanket' (that is, that they were the children born of their mother's adulterous relationship), and therefore doomed. However, while Nisien was a benign peacemaker, his brother, Efnisien, was the opposite. He was a troublemaker, a warmonger and a murderer. And it was Efnisien who was the catalyst in the story and whose actions in insulting the Irish king, Matholwch, caused the catastrophic war between Wales and Ireland. I can't help wondering whether this particular story in the Second Branch might have had some foundation in genuine ancient conflict between the two nations.

Not only was Efnisien guilty of warmongering, but he was also guilty of infanticide. He was still incandescent with rage over Branwen's marriage to Matholwch even after peace had been agreed between the armies of Wales and Ireland. During the feast that was held at the investiture of the royal couple's young son, Gwern, as future ruler of Ireland, Efnisien seized him and cast him into the hearth to be burnt alive in the fire, thus setting the two kingdoms at war once again. But even Efnisien, the black sheep, eventually redeemed himself, at the cost of his own life when he immolated himself in Brân's infamous cauldron, thereby paying his debt to Wales for causing the calamitous war with Ireland. Does an essentially Christian message lurk behind this part of the story of Brân? Was Efnisien a kind of Judas figure, whose actions led to catastrophe, and who then killed himself in remorse for his evil deeds?

Gender wars in the Fourth Branch

It is in the Fourth Branch of the *Mabinogi* that gender conflicts become an essential feature of the storyteller's narrative. In some ways, this mythical tale of Math and his people is the most complex of the Four Branches. Right at the beginning, we are presented with the weird figure of Math, his power emanating from the virgin in whose lap his feet had to stay unless he was away at war. Goewin's maiden status was crucial to him because it represented sexuality in its purest, undissipated form, presumably because of the complete, unshared strength contained within this chaste woman. We are immediately faced with a curious dichotomy in the relationship between Math and Goewin: there is an intimacy in the foot-holding yet they are sexually distant. It is the breaching of that contained virginity that leads to a complex series of calamities that beset the kingdom of Gwynedd. And this sets the scene for the 'battle of the sexes', a theme that pervades the whole story of this northern chiefdom.

Once Math's nephew, the magician Gwydion, persuaded his uncle into waging war with Dyfed in order to acquire the enchanted pigs that Arawn had presented as a gift to Pryderi, everything began to unravel. For Math released Goewin from her duties in order to lead his warriors into battle, thus clearing the way for Gwydion's brother, Gilfaethwy, to seduce and defile her, rendering her redundant as Math's foot-holder. This piece of mischief forced Math to seek another candidate for the post. And so Aranrhod ('silver wheel') was introduced into the story. She turned out to be a destructive force in the land, for she failed Math's virginity test by producing a pair of infants: Dylan, who disappeared into the sea and was later murdered, and a second son, on whom his resentful mother laid her three injunctions (or curses). Not only did she deny him a name and his right to receive arms upon reaching puberty, but she also prohibited him from marrying, thus ensuring the end of her line. Why she did this is not made clear. Was it shame at her apparent promiscuity, or revenge on the child that lost her the vital role that had been Goewin's? Whatever the reason – and we can imagine how this enigma might have been chewed over by early listeners to the tales – this second boy seems to have been doomed from the start to be the victim of cruel women. Even though

Gwydion was able to wield his magical powers successfully in order that the child could be named – Lleu Llaw Gyffes ('fair one of the skilful hand') – and he tricked Aranrhod into inadvertently giving him arms, he still could not avert the disaster that befell this hapless youth.

The second female figure to blight Lleu's life was Blodeuwedd, the 'flower-woman'. The three flowers chosen by Gwydion (and Math) to conjure Lleu's wife were those of the oak, meadowsweet and broom. These are flowers that each come into bloom at a different time of the year and, perhaps, they were so selected to represent the whole year and thus to provide this unstable 'woman' with particular power. Was it because of her peculiar, non-human beginnings that she had no morals and showed her 'lack of moral fibre' through her faithlessness and the incitement to the murder of her husband? Blodeuwedd was a pawn in Gwydion's game and, in a sense, she could also be viewed as a victim. And Lleu – perhaps himself also of magical origin, since he apparently had no father – showed a certain weakness or at least a lack of shrewdness, in happily entrusting his errant wife with the details of how his death might be brought about, in spite of Gwydion's protective spells.

The storyteller presented the possibility of Lleu's 'impossible death' in the form of a riddle. Riddles go back a very long way in myths and magic: indeed they might almost be perceived as sacred word games, with rules that had to be obeyed. A good example of this is in J. R. R. Tolkien's classic fantasy, *The Hobbit*, where the eponymous Bilbo Baggins encountered the creature Gollum, who dwelt underground, and made a bargain with him, so that whoever won the riddle-game had his wish granted. If Bilbo won, then Gollum would show him the way out of the subterranean maze, while Gollum's victory would result in the killing (and grisly consumption) of the hobbit. After some verbal sparring, Bilbo is worrying about which riddle he can ask, when he fondles a ring he found and has placed in his pocket. He vaguely asks aloud, 'What do I have in my pocket?' Gollum assumes this is the riddle and is driven to anger by his inability to answer. Then Gollum realises that Bilbo has found his 'precious': the magic gold ring he had strangled his cousin to obtain, and the One Ring destined by the evil Sauron, the necromancer, to be used to destroy the world of good and flood it with malevolence.

Blodeuwedd managed to tempt Lleu to reveal the answer to the riddle surrounding his own mortality. As is often the case with riddles, the number three held particular magic for there were three standards that needed to be met for Lleu to die. Lleu first explained that 'unless God [the Christian God] slay me, it is not easy to slay me'. He then described, in great detail, to his treacherous wife, that he could only be killed with a special weapon: a spear that would take a year to forge, and could only be worked upon when people were at Mass on a Sunday. Secondly, Lleu explained that he could not be killed either inside or outside a house. And thirdly, that he could neither meet his end on horseback nor on foot. When Blodeuwedd asked him by what manner he *could* be killed, he naïvely says: 'by making a bath for me on a river bank, and making a vaulted frame over the tub, and thatching it well … and after bringing a he-goat, said he, and setting it beside the tub, and myself placing one foot on the back of the he-goat and the other on the edge of the tub. Whoever should smite me when so, he would bring about my death.' Blodeuwedd replied that she was relieved and grateful to God for making her husband's death impossible, while signalling to her lover, Gronw, that he should begin to make ready for Lleu's murder.

The punishment inflicted by Math upon his errant nephews, Gwydion and Gilfaethwy was all to do with transformation-magic: doubly powerful because it not only manipulated human and animal species but also gender. Math chose this latter element because the crimes committed by the pair were centred upon and ended with Gilfaethwy's non-consensual congress with the virgin, Goewin. It was an act of betrayal that threatened to rob the king of Gwynedd of his very power to rule. So, in a sense, Gilfaethwy's lust and his brother Gwydion's connivance did double violence: both to Math and (as collateral damage) to his foot-holder. Goewin's role – though understated in the story – was an important one. Upon her undissipated sexual potency rested the whole power base of the land, so it is valid to see the relationship between Math and Goewin in terms of a kind of sexual union, though not in the accepted sense of consummated marriage.

The theme of gender wars is aptly played out in Math's revenge on his perfidious nephews Gwydion and Gilfaethwy. The 'changing-spell' he cast upon them messed with their identities as 'heroes' in human form by not only by turning them into beasts of the wild but also by swapping their genders. Moreover, the spell impelled the brothers to have sexual congress with each other, so committing incest and thereby putting them even further beyond the pale of 'normal'. The brothers even have issue of their sexual congress – three sons:

'The three sons of false Gilfaethwy,
Three champions true,
Bleiddwn [wolf], Hyddwn [stag] and Hychdwn Hir [tall pig].'

This gender-bending episode is interesting, for it is part of a whole raft of references to gender-reversal or gender-mixing in other mythologies. For example, in the Irish tale of 'Da Derga's Hostel', the Irish king Conaire Mór encountered the Irish battle/death-goddess, the Badbh, who appears as a bearded woman. In *Macbeth*, Shakespeare's witches wore beards to add to the horror of their appearance. Might this have been based on earlier tales of supernatural gender-morphing? All of these 'special' women emanated from the otherworld, which is where the human world could be warped and disfigured and where the values of earthly existence were null and void.

The question of Arthur

We have briefly come across Arthur already in the tale of 'Culhwch and Olwen'. I should emphasise that, although there are a number of tales about Arthur, the best-known were the Arthurian 'legends' and were written by a French author of medieval romance, Chrétien de Troyes. So the stories of Arthur's knights, his Round Table, his quest for the Holy Grail, and his death and carriage to Avalon all belong to medieval French romance literature rather than Welsh mythology. However, he is presented as a larger-than-life hero in Welsh legend through his knights, many of whom are displayed as possessing super-human abilities, such as impressive battle skills, magical weapons, the capacity to do without breath or sleep for days on end, and the ability

PLAYING WITH GENDER
AND SPECIES IN ANCIENT IMAGERY

There is a body of firm evidence for gender-ambiguity in later prehistoric and Roman period iconography in Britain and Europe, and some examples of the morphing of human and animal form. The custom of disrupting norms is frequently expressed, for instance, on Iron Age coins where the boundaries between both gender and species of images could be fuzzy and contradictory. Some late Iron Age Breton coins figure a horsewoman brandishing weapons, riding a human-headed horse. Another coin, from Bratislava, Slovakia, displays a galloping horse whose gender is deliberately ambiguous: jutting beneath its belly are three excrescencies that represent either triple penises or triple teats. A Gallo-Roman figurine from Gaul (unprovenanced) depicts a seated woman wearing the antlers of a male red deer. And these are just a few of many such gender or species twists that exhibit fluidity and boundary-crossing a thousand years or so before the Welsh myths were committed to writing but – just possibly – might have remained in long ancestral memory.

to speak all languages – even those of beasts. In the story of the quest to track down the beautiful Olwen for his cousin, Culhwch, Arthur often invoked (the Christian) God as his source of strength. Yet, interwoven with Christian references, are relics of paganism, such as wondrous animals and magical objects like swords and cauldrons. One of the 'labours' demanded of Culhwch, which Arthur undertook, was to steal a cauldron owned by an Irishman called Diwrnach. It was a magic vessel containing all the treasures of Ireland. Arthur made the journey across the Irish Sea to obtain the cauldron and its contents and, after engaging in a bitter battle with the Irish, came back to Wales with the prize.

The mention of cauldrons – and cauldron-rustling – brings me to another Welsh mythic tale associated with Arthur. It is an early poem contained within the *Book of Taliesin* (a collection of poems compiled in the early medieval period). The poem is called *Preiddeu Annwfn* (*The Spoils of Annwfn*), and it tells a story that paints Arthur in a less than honourable light. Rather like his adventure in Ireland, Arthur, like Pwyll in the First Branch, made a journey to Annwfn, the Welsh otherworld, to procure another cauldron. But – as one might expect for an object belonging to the spirit world of the dead – this cauldron possessed its own capricious personality: it refused to boil food for a coward and required the breath of nine virgins to keep its fire going so as to heat the broth therein. As with Diwrnach's cauldron, Arthur paid dearly for this otherworldly vessel, with a war that left most of his warriors slaughtered on the battlefield.

So the Welsh Arthur comes across as quite a different character from the noble, honour-driven hero of Chrétien de Troyes's romances. In the mythic stories of Wales, Arthur was presented, at least in part, as a swashbuckling brigand, spoiling for a fight, putting his men in peril, and stealing. *Preiddeu Annwfn* is interesting, though, because it ties Arthur into the genre of the 'hero' who ventured into the otherworld while still alive and bravely faced the extreme hazards that went with such a challenge.

Before we leave Arthur, there is a quirky link between the Welsh legends of his exploits and the French medieval romances, written by Chrétien, that we should explore. In the latter narrative, Arthur's Round Table, around which Arthur and his knights gathered to discuss affairs of state, was described in detail; but one of the stories included in the eleven tales constituting the *Mabinogion*, entitled 'Peredur, son of Efrog', placed Arthur's court at Caerleon – the site of the Roman legionary fortress, with its oval amphitheatre that some narrators associated with the famous Arthurian Round Table.

The great enchanted wild boar, Twrch Trwyth,
with his comb, razor and shears on his back.

CHAPTER 3

Fabulous Beasts
and Shape-shifters

*And having recovered their strength and their magic powers,
in rage and exultation the ravens straightway swooped down to
earth upon the men who had earlier inflicted hurt and injury
and loss upon them. Of some they were carrying off the heads,
of others the eyes, of others the ears, and of others the arms ...*

This quotation comes, not from one of the Four Branches, but from one other of the eleven tales that also make up the *Mabinogion*: 'Rhonabwy's Dream'. The 'hero' of the tale, Rhonabwy, lay down to sleep but, unlike his companions, he could not get comfortable, so he decided to lie down upon a yellow ox-skin in the hope that it would lull him to sleep. I wonder whether this is significant, because in Greek mythology, ox-skins were deemed to act as corridors to the spirit world. It is possible that the storyteller (or at least the person who wrote the tale down) was familiar with the Classics and wove it into their narrative. The skin-blanket works and Rhonabwy experiences a complicated dream of Arthur, who is preoccupied with a game of *gwyddbwyll*, a board game not unlike chess; he is playing with one of his followers, a man named Owain, son of Urien. Anything is possible in a dream world and the storyteller introduced a friction between Arthur's retinue and Owain's in the form of a quarrel over a hostile act on the part of Arthur's champions, who were harming Owain's flock of magical ravens. After several episodes of harrying these birds, the tables

RAVENS AND SHAMANS

Because of their intelligence, their propensity to pick up human speech, and their own distinctive 'voices', it is unsurprising that in some societies, including those of medieval Ireland, ravens came to be associated with shape-shifting – usually between bird and human form. There is a tiny piece of evidence from two pre-Roman Iron Age archaeological sites in southern Britain that could suggest the existence of rituals or ceremonies, perhaps associated with shamanism, that made use of skin-turning imagery. Deep pits at both these sites contained animal body-parts, almost all from domestic animals, which would almost certainly have been ritual offerings. But an exception was the presence of ravens' remains, because nearly all of these were from elderly birds, suggesting that they might have been kept as 'pets'. But the most remarkable feature of these skeletons is the presence of deliberate cut-marks that betray the probable harvest of wings and feathers, as if they were taken to adorn headdresses or costumes. It is possible that the individuals who wore such costumes were shamans, people who were recognised as having the ability to take 'soul-flight' between the material and spirit worlds in order to liaise with the gods. In many societies, past and present, shamans would don animal skins, horns or feathers in order to facilitate their ability to shape-change, thus enabling access to other dimensions and communication with gods and ancestors on behalf of their communities.

were suddenly turned, which resulted in Arthur's men being bloodily routed by Owain's birds. 'Rhonabwy's Dream' is full of otherworld references, including the appearance of riders on strangely-coloured horses. As elsewhere in Welsh myth, the colour red plays a prominent part in hinting at otherworld presences in this tale.

Ravens inspire stories in many mythic traditions. They are large, glossy-black, carrion-eaters, with a singular call and – like crows – they are highly intelligent and excellent problem-solvers. They can be taught to speak and are sometimes associated with the ability to foretell the future. In Irish mythology, ravens haunted battlefields, feeding on the slain. In the early medieval Ulster myth, '*Táin Bó Cuailnge*' ('The Cattle Raid of Cooley'), the hero Cú Chulainn had many encounters with ravens, in particular the shape-shifting raven-goddess, the Badbh, a war-deity who both aided and then ultimately betrayed him in his final fight for Ulster against Connacht and its fearsome queen Medbh (Maeve).

Rhonabwy's dream or vision might be interpreted in terms of a residual tradition in which skin-turning was part of spiritual life and a means of tapping into the otherworld. Owain's ravens were clearly special, with particular skills and properties outside the avian norm. And, like the ravens and raven goddesses of early Ireland, they were closely associated with battle and slaughter. Were they skin-turners who changed shape between human and raven? Clearly a raven of normal size could not hope to take on a grown man in battle and tear him to pieces.

Blurring boundaries

Myths, by their very nature, stretch and break through 'normal', human-centred barriers. We have already witnessed this in earlier chapters: superhuman heroes such as Brân and Rhiannon, and objects with peculiar properties, like the cauldron of rebirth. Culhwch's quest for his sweetheart, Olwen, was only successful because of assistance from larger-than-life animals with special powers, and his story revolves around a quest to find a giant boar, transformed from his human self. Now we're going to explore, in greater depth, the whole issue of flouting boundaries, norms and barriers, particularly those associated with

THE SIGNIFICANCE OF BOARD GAMES

Before we leave Rhonabwy and his dream, there is one other element that deserves a mention: the board game played by Arthur and Owain. Evidence from antiquity indicates that such games sometimes possessed a quasi-religious function in themselves. Some graves from early Roman Britain contained game boards and counters. One particular tomb stands out: the so-called 'Doctor's Grave', which was found in Stanway just outside Colchester in Essex. The man's tomb contained a surgical kit and a set of divining rods, all laid out on a board with blue and white counters. The most striking thing, though, was the position of the counters which implied a game was mid-play, as if two players were present. Could the person buried in this grave have been a shaman in life – a 'two-spirit' individual who dwelt on earth but was able to travel to other worlds?

shape-changing and with supernaturally charged beasts.

In the Welsh myths, shape-changing between human and animal was either voluntary or imposed in retribution for misconduct. In the tale of Ceridwen's cauldron, the little boy, Gwion, who unwittingly stole Afagddu's inheritance (the knowledge and wisdom to be gained from his mother's magic brew), fled from Ceridwen's wrath by turning himself into various creatures. She, in turn, kept up the pursuit by changing into predatory animals in order to murder him. The story reached its conclusion when Gwion eventually changed into a grain of corn, only to be swallowed by Ceridwen, who had transformed into a hen. He was then reborn as Taliesin. So, in this tale, the shape-shifting was a voluntary act for both Ceridwen and Gwion, although the boy's multiple transitions happened under duress.

Several interesting strands emanate from this story. Firstly, despite her magical, witch-like skills, Ceridwen did not possess the power to reverse Afagddu's fate after Gwion ingested her magical stew. Secondly, the shape-changing that occurred in the pursuit of Gwion had a specific pattern: whatever form Gwion took to evade capture, Ceridwen matched it by turning into an appropriate predator, and each subsequent change fed into Gwion's final reincarnation. And it seems as though a power, superior to Ceridwen herself, was pulling the strings in order that her wisdom-rich quarry should survive and blossom as the shaman-poet Taliesin ('the shining one').

Punishment and rescue: animal-transformers

What is abundantly clear is that most, if not all, of the shape-changing episodes in the Welsh myths happen within the context of the 'beyond-human' – they are driven by elements of the divine. This is most evident in the shape-changing between people and animals as retribution for wrongdoing. The punishment inflicted upon Gwydion and Gilfaethwy by Math, in the Fourth Branch, may be seen as particularly fitting: because they were responsible for Goewin's own transformation from her virgin state, they, too, were forcibly changed. Their new state, as animals, reflected a dramatic lowering in status, and it is perhaps significant that all three animals involved – deer, wild boar and wolves – were undomesticated creatures of the wild. Their offspring, though transformed to humans, also all retained their animal-personae in their names. We know that Gwydion, at least, played a key role in the life of Lleu, later on in the story, so perhaps he was rehabilitated because he was not the brother who had actually taken away Goewin's virginity, though he had connived to facilitate her rape.

This last part of the story of Math contains more punitive shape-changing, in the fate of the fickle and feckless 'woman of flowers', Blodeuwedd. Gwydion (and Math) had created her from wild flowers, so she was already a victim of magical transformation when she was turned into an unstable human female form. Her unfaithfulness to her husband, Lleu, and her plot to bring about his death indicated that she was not worthy of her humanity, and so Gwydion used his powers as a wizard to transform her again – not back into flowers, but into an owl. And he cursed her with the added shame of being cast out from daylight and the companionship of other birds, and forced to hunt in solitary stealth by night. It is interesting that, in this tale, the owl was presented as a personification of evil, while the tale of 'Culhwch and Olwen' contains a reference to an owl of great wisdom. This is one of many wondrous creatures that helped the questers to find Mabon and, ultimately, Olwen herself.

In 'Culhwch and Olwen', we are not told what evil deed(s) Twrch Trwyth and his followers were guilty of, but they were considered to have warranted their transformation into ferocious wild boars. These creatures retained their original minds and knew full well that their new state had been brought about by their wickedness. And, unlike the revenge wreaked upon Math's errant nephews, the storyteller made it clear that divine (Christian divine) intervention had demanded their transference from human to animal form. It seems, from Twrch Trwyth's confession, that he was not only aware of his sins but that he regretted them.

At the beginning of Culhwch's story, he was instructed by his father to visit his cousin Arthur and to request him to trim his hair for him. The act of cutting someone's hair was perceived as recognition of kinship, and so it is highly significant in terms of the boy's legitimate claim to his senior cousin's help in his quest for Olwen. The cutting of the boy's hair may also have symbolised Culhwch's coming of age and, by this grooming act, Arthur may have been giving the youth his blessing and recognition of his manhood. Ysbaddaden seems to have had a fixation with his hair and beard. In one of the earlier tasks he demanded the acquisition of the tusk of another boar, 'White Tusk, Chief of Boars', in order that the giant could shave his beard. The tusk had to be pulled from the boar's jaw while it was still living – a momentous task indeed!

The hair symbolism continued throughout the saga, in the most curious and bizarre aspect of the boar's narrative: the need for Culhwch to overcome him and to extract the comb, razor and shears from between Twrch Trwyth's ears. This was the ultimate 'labour' that

Culhwch had to undergo in order to claim his bride, Olwen. What is this all about? And why was this so important to Ysbaddaden? There is another dimension to the significance of hair-grooming equipment here, and it is one that may stretch back as far as Iron Age traditions. Culhwch's request for Arthur to cut his hair was not only symbolic of their familial relationship but it involved some ceremony, for Arthur did not just seize any comb and shears but used 'a golden comb, and shears with loops of silver'. Is there, therefore, a hint in this story of an understanding that this transformed boar, more powerful than any other, was seen by the giant, Ysbaddaden, as some kind of kin?

Shape-changing in Welsh myths was not always punitive. We have seen that Gwion's multiple transformations, even though he underwent them in order to elude the wrath of Ceridwen, enabled him, ultimately, to be reborn. At the end of the story of Math, Lleu's death from Gronw's spear did not result in a human corpse but in Lleu's transformation into the form of an eagle, which flew, screeching, to the top of a mighty oak tree. The storyteller then reveals the grisly image of this great bird, sitting in the tree as his body rotted, shedding decaying flesh and maggots onto the ground to be sniffed out, with relish, by a sow. But it was this rotting flesh that secured his salvation, for it allowed Gwydion to track him down by following the sow. After this, he was reborn into his old self although, perhaps, not the same as he had been before calamity overtook him. As related earlier in this volume, Lleu's transition to an eagle may owe something to earlier religious tradition in Roman Britain and Western Europe, where the sky-god (the Roman Jupiter and the Gallo-British Taranis) was associated with eagles. Both are also closely linked to oak trees. Lleu's name evokes celestial symbolism, so his ultimately pagan roots may be reflected not only in his shape-change but also his sojourn in the sky-god's lofty oak – its branches reaching up to touch the heavens.

Wondrous beasts

A persistent thread running through many Welsh mythic tales is the porosity of boundaries between spirits and people and between people and animals. For instance, Pwyll, lord of Arberth, encountered the white, red-eared otherworldly hounds of Arawn, and he witnessed the appearance of Rhiannon on her shining white horse, which no earthly rider could outpace.

It is clear from repeated references that Rhiannon herself had an equine persona. She first erupts into Welsh myth as the rider on the horse that could not be outrun. Her kidnapped baby son, Pryderi, was swapped for a newborn colt, and Rhiannon was twice punished by being treated as a beast of burden, first by her husband Pwyll (in the First Branch) and then by the bishop-sorcerer who imprisoned her and her son in his enchanted castle (in the Third Branch). So it is easy to see Rhiannon as possessing links with the ancient horse-goddess

THE LANGUAGE OF HAIR
IN ANCIENT BRITAIN AND GAUL

Hair-grooming equipment does not simply tidy people up; it transforms their appearance. Hairstyles hold cultural significance all over the world, and the same is true of their significance in the past. Hair (or its absence) makes statements about who we are and how we wish to be perceived. From shaven heads to dreadlocks and from vivid dyes to quiffs, the world of hair remains redolent with meaning to this day.

So it is no surprise to find copious evidence from Iron Age and Roman provincial contexts for the deposition of tweezers, razors, shears and combs in shrines and inside graves. The well-preserved, late Iron Age bog body from Cheshire, known as Lindow Man, had had his moustache trimmed with a razor just prior to his death. Another body, found in a rich inhumation grave from Saint-Georges-lès-Baillargeaux in southern France, dating to the late pre-Roman period, was accompanied by a set of finely made bronze razors. And an early Romano-British ritual deposit at the watery site of Flag Fen in Cambridgeshire revealed a pair of bronze shears placed in a custom-made box, as a gift to the gods. The well-known gilded silver cauldron found at Gundestrup in Jutland, Denmark, was probably made in about 100 BC, and is covered with images of sacred scenes and divine figures. One panel shows the head and shoulders of a woman having her hair braided by two acolytes or servants. Hair was special; head hair and facial hair conveyed important messages concerning gender, age and status. There is evidence that the tools that governed its transformation were also imbued with gravitas and symbolism for many centuries before the Welsh myths were written down. Maybe some of this earlier significance to hair and grooming tools left its imprint on the Welsh oral tradition and wove its way into the myths.

Epona, whose sacred images in Roman Gaul and Britain depict her riding a mare, often with a foal curled up beneath her body.

The magical character of wild animals is especially prominent in the story of 'Culhwch and Olwen', where Arthur and Culhwch set out to find Mabon the divine hunter so that he could help them track down the great boar Twrch Trwyth. The heroes' desperation to discover Mabon's whereabouts led them to seek aid from a range of wild beasts and birds, all of whom were described as the oldest (and, by implication, therefore the wisest) animals in the world. One of Arthur's men, Gwrhyr, played a crucial role here in that only he could speak to these creatures in their own languages. Each of the beasts was tied to a particular place. And as the story develops, a pattern emerges: each animal they approached said that the only way he or she could help was to refer Arthur and Culhwch's men to a beast created by God even earlier than themselves.

The first was the Blackbird of Cilgwri (suggested as being the Wirral Peninsula). She informed Gwrhyr that she would help in the quest and that she would lead the company to an even older creature that had been made by God before she was created. This was the Stag of Rhedynfre (tentatively identified as being Farndon, near the Wirral).

The Stag had a brief, but interesting, story to tell about himself: when he first arrived at his dwelling place, he only had a single antler on each side of his head (this demonstrated his youth, as a fully grown, alpha-male stag might have fourteen tines). He went on to describe how, at first, there was only one tree, an oak sapling that eventually grew so large that it had a hundred branches (a clue to indicate its advanced age). Beneath his words, there lurks an inference that the Stag and the tree were closely knit together and that their fortunes marched alongside each other. The oak died, said the Stag and, though it is not mentioned in so many words, this was why he remained 'frozen in time' in the very spot that he first remembered inhabiting. But now, Gwrhyr's plea for help had persuaded the Stag to be the company's guide, and he took them to meet an older and wiser creature still, the Owl of Cwm Cawlwyd (which is perhaps somewhere near Llanrwst, in Gwynedd). It was a revered and ancient creature, very different from the bird into which the shamed Blodeuwedd was transformed under Gwydion's curse.

The Owl of Cwm Cawlwyd told Gwrhyr that he should converse with the 'very oldest animal in the world', namely the Eagle of Gwernabwy (a location possibly somewhere in the Llŷn Peninsula). The eagle had a dramatic tale to tell of another creature that might be able to help Arthur and Culhwch, the great Salmon of Llyn Llyw (a lake that has been suggested as being somewhere around the Severn Estuary). The eagle was out hunting fish one day and managed to bury its talons in the back of a large salmon. But the eagle had underestimated the strength of the fish. The bird held on even while being pulled under the water by the strength of its quarry. The salmon eventually breaks free from the bird's clutches. The eagle was so incensed that it called upon all its fellow eagles to hunt out and destroy the salmon, but the latter was a wise fish and it sent messengers to solicit for peace. The salmon had an ulterior motive, for it came to its former pursuer and asked the bird to remove fifty tridents (three-pronged spears) that were embedded in its back from the blows of many fishermen. The eagle was impressed by the great salmon's wisdom, as well as its strength and courage, and so the two became allies. And it was the salmon, the wisest creature in the world, that Arthur's messengers were recommended to find, as it was the creature most likely to be able to find Mabon.

The salmon is a strange and rather wonderful fish, and stories about its magical properties are present in both Welsh and Irish mythologies. I suspect that one reason for this is connected to the salmon's strange and complex life cycle. They are born and spend their juvenile phase in fresh-water rivers, before they then migrate to the sea, reaching their maturity there. They start life in slow-moving upper rivers and, as they develop, they swim down to the fast-flowing lower water prior to making their way to the sea to live their adult lives until they return to lay their eggs. Atlantic salmon (the species associated with the Irish Sea) spend their whole lives there until they return to their exact birthplace to spawn and die in their home river. But their journey to their spawning-grounds is dramatic, for they have to swim upstream from the lower river, leaping several metres into the air and often seeming to take to the air in flight, in order to reach the 'nursery' of the upper river. The complicated life cycle of salmon, and their unerring ability to navigate to the sea and then to return after many years to their birthplaces, must have fired the imagination of storytellers and encouraged them to portray the creatures as endowed with magical wisdom and knowledge. The life of the salmon, with its freshwater and saltwater affinities, plus the apparent ability to 'fly' up-river, gave it particular richness in symbolism. And another aspect of this fish that, perhaps, fed into its special status in Welsh and Irish mythology, is the pink colouring of its flesh, due to its diet of krill and shrimp. This may have been perceived as signifying an affinity between the salmon and humans.

After the Eagle of Gwernabwy had introduced Gwrhyr and his Arthurian companions to the Salmon of Llyn Llyw, in the hope that it could help them locate Mabon, the fish explained that (unlike salmon in real life) every flood tide, it swam up the Severn until it arrived at Gloucester Castle (Caer Loyw). It told the men that this was the wickedest place he had ever come across. The Salmon was so huge that it was able to carry Gwrhyr and another of Arthur's men, Cei, to the castle walls, where they heard the sound of lamentation within. It was Mabon, crying out his anguish at being imprisoned in the castle. His plight was reported back to Arthur and his army and they stormed the castle and released Mabon. So it was the salmon, with its knowledge, that provided the turning point in the story of 'Culhwch and Olwen', ultimately allowing the company to track down the elusive Twrch Trwyth and therefore to fulfil Ysbaddaden's final and trickiest demand for the hair-grooming set borne by the giant boar.

In Irish mythology, the theme of the Salmon of Knowledge developed in a different direction from the Welsh tradition. In the early medieval texts of the Fenian Cycle, the narrative explores the life of the eponymous hero, Finn. A central part of his story is his acquisition of knowledge from the Salmon of Wisdom. This remarkable fish dwelt in a pool within the ocean, and it had received its all-knowing powers from ingesting nuts from nine magical hazel trees that grew on the sea-floor. One day, a bard named Finnegas was fishing in the pool for this secretive creature who had eluded capture by him for seven years, when the young Finn approached. Finnegas then, finally, caught the salmon and cooked its flesh over a fire, commanding Finn to watch over the cooking but warning him not to touch its flesh. Readers will note a resonance between this tale and the story of Ceridwen's cauldron and the young boy Gwion's accidental ingestion of knowledge from its contents. While supervising the cooking fire, Finn's thumb touched the scorching flesh of the fish and he, instinctively, sucked the sore spot. As he did so, he acquired the salmon's wisdom and the gift of prophecy besides. It is clear from narratives such as this that there was active cross-fertilisation between Welsh and Irish storytelling traditions, which suggests that itinerant yarn-spinners travelled widely, crossing the Irish Sea in both directions to disseminate these strange and evocative tales.

SALMON MYTHS ON SCOTTISH STONES?

The Pictish people, whose lands stretched from the rivers Forth and Clyde up to the far north of Scotland and the Northern Isles, carved enigmatic images on stone mono-liths (symbol stones) in the early medieval period, between the fifth and ninth centuries AD. While not wishing to speculate too wildly, I find it interesting that some of the motifs on these stones bear resemblances to certain Welsh mythic tales. One of these is the salmon, and others portray grooming-articles such as combs and mirrors. These motifs are repeated on several of the stones, and at least two of them are found on the same stone. For example, a symbol stone at Aberlemno in Angus carries designs of a salmon and a mirror. It also, interestingly, features what is general-ly interpreted as a snake but what seems, to me, more likely to represent an eel (a creature that, like the salmon, has a complex life cycle that involves 'homing'). It is prudent to be careful not to read too much into apparent resonances with Welsh mythic themes. There is a wide range of sym-bols on the Scottish stones, most of which are peculiar to these artefacts. But is it too far-fetched to imagine that the repeated motifs just mentioned may have some elements related to Welsh mythic tradition?

Whiffs of shamanism

Underlying the persistent blurring of boundaries between deities, people and animals in the Welsh tales are hints of shamanic presences. Shape-shifting is a central tenet of shamanism, and many branches of traditional religion, past and present, embrace the notion that ritual practitioners use skin-turning to move their souls between the material and spirit worlds. In communities that practise shamanism, animals are regarded as having particular powers to access the otherworld and are seen as go-betweens that allow human shamans to consult with spirit forces and thus advise their people on important matters such as healing and crop-growth. In this way, shamans gain their reputation as seers or prophets who can ascertain the will of the spirits and act as envoys between worlds. It is possible that the shape-shifters and magical animals in the Welsh myths contain remnants of this ancient shamanism.

Archaeological footprints of shamanism

A wealth of iconography has been left by communities living in later prehistoric and Roman Europe, and some of it raises questions as to whether it indicates the existence of shamanic ritual and spirituality. Very striking examples include some of the later Bronze Age rock-carvings from Scandinavia, which include horned or winged human figures. And another pocket of relevant rock-art was found in a valley in northern Italy: Val Camonica, not far from Bologna. Dating from the Iron Age (about the fifth century BC) to the Roman occupation of this region (late first century BC), these rock carvings include images of figures that are half-stag, half-human. The valley itself formed a natural corridor for the migration of herds, and the images of alpha-male deer (with enormous, multi-tined antlers) and the man/stag depictions may have had connections with hunting. This specific combination of stag/human images recurs in the late Iron Age and Roman periods in Gaul and Britannia. One of the most evocative of these was carved on an image-rich stone column in Paris in the early first century AD. The carving depicts the head of a man sprouting red deer antlers with two necklets (torcs) hanging from the tines. The god's name, Cernunnos (meaning 'horned' or 'peaked' one), is inscribed above the antlered head.

This stag/human imagery is sometimes represented with other species. In several depictions, the Cernunnos figure is associated with another strange creature: a serpent with a ram's horns. Such iconography exhibits an intensifying of shape-shifting that chimes with the dualities expressed in the mythic tales of Wales. Snakes are associated with 'rebirth' because of their skin-shedding, so it is not so surprising that they are often seen as special creatures, with a spiritual dimension. So what might these hybrid forms actually mean in terms of shamanism? One plausible theory, to which I subscribe, is that such images represent a 'freeze-frame' – a capturing of the very instant of change between human and animal, so that both forms are reflected at the moment of transformation.

The shape-shifting exhibited in the sacred imagery of late Iron Age and Roman period Western Europe may have its roots in societies where shamanistic transition was a key element in the perceived relationships between people and the gods. Religious beliefs here seem – from the iconography and (in the Roman period) epigraphy at least – to have been predicated upon the natural world and the sanctity of landscapes. The same appears to have been true, to an extent, of underlying themes within the Welsh myths. Animals, both in their natural and shape-changed states, played crucial parts both in the overt paganism of Iron Age and Roman Britain and in Welsh mythology. Similarly, the emphasis on natural places – rivers, forests and lakes – may be mapped in both archaeology and myth, despite their chronological disparity.

Shamanic aspects of the Welsh myths

It is necessary to dig deep in order to try and identify possible remnants of shamanistic traditions within the Welsh myths. But I am sure that they are present and contributed to the abundance of shape-changing and of transgressing thresholds between humans, animals and spirits in the stories.

Rhiannon is a prime example of that bridge between identities. She was a human woman but inextricably linked to horses, as was her son, Pryderi. Her first appearance to Pwyll while he sat upon his magic mound confirms this link. And the seeds of wonder sown by the storyteller at this point also confirm her magical status.

The character of Gwydion, with his powers of wizardry, is another case in point. He and his uncle, Math, created a woman from flowers, something only possible with magical aid. And Gwydion's protection of Lleu is further evidence that he possesses peculiar, shamanic powers. It is perhaps permissible to see his hand in Lleu's transformation from dying man to eagle, and certainly in the magical *englyn* (song) used to coax the stricken bird out of the oak tree so he could be restored back to his human self.

Other examples of human/animal blurring may also have their origins within memories of shamanism that would have reached back in the oral tradition of storytelling. One of the most powerful and enduring is the tale of Culhwch in which pigs featured strongly, both in the circumstances of his birth and also in the persona of what might easily be viewed as his nemesis: Twrch Trwyth, the former king who had been changed into a giant boar as a punishment for his evil ways. And might Arthur's man, Gwrhyr, have had his origins in shamanism? His ability to speak, like Dr Dolittle, to wild animals strikes a chord with the widespread shamanic tradition of 'animal helpers' – creatures that facilitated the transference of human shamans to the world of the spirit. In the Welsh myths, animals frequently showed the way to the otherworld. It happened to Pwyll, when his hounds encountered those of Arawn, and it occurred again when a shining white boar lured Rhiannon and Pryderi to the magic castle, where they were immured until the spell was broken.

Finally, we can't leave this chapter on shape-shifting without considering the magic number three, to which frequent allusion is made in the Welsh mythic tradition. The number three is especially relevant to shamanism. Many present-day shamans (for instance those in Siberia) have a belief that the world is a 'triple-layered cosmos'. The universe is divided into three layers: an underworld for the dead; the middle layer of the material world inhabited by living people, animals and the natural environment; and, above, a layer that is the dwelling place of the spirits. It would be crass to impose such a model on the myths of Wales. However, the number three appears to have been an important element in the stories. For example, in the Second Branch of the *Mabinogion*, Branwen is described as one of the three 'chief maidens' of the land. There are three singing birds of Rhiannon, the magical creatures mentioned in the Second Branch and in the tale of 'Culhwch and Olwen', that have magical powers to wake the dead and send the living to sleep. And the link between Rhiannon and these birds is significant for it reinforces the idea that this woman has issued from the otherworld.

Why does triplism play such a key role in the Welsh myths? Three-ness is a persistent trope in so many cultures, past and present. Like many Welsh mythic themes, the idea of supernatural birds from the otherworld occurs also in the Irish tradition. To pluck a few examples from near home: Shakespeare's witches in *Macbeth* were a trio. There are three blind mice in the old nursery rhyme. We are granted three wishes by a genie. And we raise three cheers to someone whom we are celebrating. The significance of number is explored more deeply in a later chapter.

Dead warriors emerge reborn after
being dipped into Brân's cauldron.

CHAPTER 4

Otherworlds and Immortality

Pwyll made for the court. And in the court he could see sleeping-rooms and halls and chambers and the greatest show of buildings any one had ever seen. And he went into the hall to pull off his boots. There came squires and chamberlains to pull them off him, and all as they came saluted him. Two knights came to rid him of his hunting garb and to apparel him in a robe of gold brocaded silk. And the hall was made ready. Here he could see a war-band and retinues entering in, and the most comely troop and the best equipped any one had seen ... And they passed their time with meat and drink and song and carousal. Of all the courts he had seen on earth, that was the court best furnished with meat and drink and vessels of gold and royal jewels.

This quotation, from the First Branch of the *Mabinogi*, describes the otherworld kingdom of Annwfn that Pwyll visited after his agreement with its lord, Arawn, that he should change places with him for a year. The most striking element is that the description bears a close resemblance to any medieval royal court in the world of living humans, and yet, that it was far more lavish than anything Pwyll had ever seen on earth. Eating, drinking, partying, hunting, dressing up in fine clothes – all these activities were enjoyed in a parallel universe. Most interesting of all is that Annwfn was described as being just like the good life on earth, only far better. As we will see later, this idea of a mythic otherworld chimes closely with others, particularly that of Ireland.

Otherworlds, underworlds and everlasting life

The otherworld of Annwfn, as described in the First Branch, was a wonderful place full of richness and fine living. The picture painted by the storyteller is very different from the sombre world of the dead imagined by so many societies, both past and present. For instance, the Hades of the classical religious tradition was a place inhabited by the wandering souls of the dead and full of vengeful spirits wreaking everlasting torture on the damned. It was an image similar to that of Milton's *Paradise Lost*, a hell into which Satan and his fellows were cast by God, with lakes of fire. In early Irish mythic tradition, spirits – often malign ones – lurked in the otherworld, ready to burst into the human world at times of the year when the threshold between them was weak and boundaries between living people and spirit forces temporarily melted away, such as Samhain. But within the same tradition, the otherworld was a wonderful place, sometimes on an enchanted island in the ocean, where people remained forever young, and filled their time hunting and feasting. But woe betide any who tried to go back to their old world on earth because, then, all the years that had passed them by in the otherworld would catch up with them and they would fall apart with extreme and instant old age. So the otherworld, for pagan Ireland, had a sting in its tail. The lesson was to abide by the rules or come to grief.

In Welsh mythology, by contrast, this kind of situation is not explicitly developed, although the appearance of otherworld creatures, such as magical wild boars who, in the Third Branch, lure the living Rhiannon and Pryderi into imprisonment in the castle, also shows the menace of the underworld. In Welsh and Irish mythology (and, to an extent, classical mythic traditions as well), there appears to be a mismatch between the ideas of 'underworld' and 'otherworld'. The question is whether they were different places. Where were the dead perceived to go after death? Were they, as in the Christian tradition, divided into those whose earthly lives were righteously lived and those who had done wicked things: the former going to live in an otherworld paradise, perhaps in the company of the spirits, and the latter damned to a miserable, pallid underworld, to wander in rejected sadness for ever?

The term 'underworld' seems to have a definite location, beneath or lower than that of earth. The idea of the 'otherworld' appears fuzzier, in terms of where it might be found, and the border between those worlds less definite. In the story of Pwyll's sojourn in Arawn's kingdom, Annwfn, it is described as being on a level with the material world, and easy to reach, with no barriers between the two. Was this ease of transition because Pwyll had been *invited* there? The storyteller makes it clear that Arawn escorted Pwyll to Annwfn's border, presumably to facilitate the earthling's entry thereto. There is a parallel between this and the journey made by the classical mythic hero, Aeneas of Troy, whose goal was to find his dead father in the underworld. Like Pwyll, Aeneas required spiritual aid: that of the Cumaean prophet, the Sibyl, who had the ear of the god Apollo. This linkage is important because the people who wrote down the Welsh tales, monks in monasteries, would have been schooled in the Classics and would have been familiar with Virgil and other great Graeco-Roman literary figures.

Another interesting element in the image of the Welsh otherworld is that it was not simply one realm. Arawn explained to Pwyll that he needed the mortal to go there in order to challenge another otherworld king, Hafgan, a rival ruler of a world next to Arawn's who was forever challenging Arawn's own authority. Here, there is no suggestion that Annwfn was the world of dead people. In Virgil's vision of the otherworld/underworld, it is clear that the dead did pass to a place beyond earth: Hades. Here they would be judged and the wicked winnowed out from the good and condemned to eternal punishment, while the souls of the righteous formed a queue to be admitted, via Charon the ferryman's boat, across the river Styx to paradise in Elysium. In the classical tradition, the otherworld was split into at least two domains.

DEATH AND AFTER-DEATH
IN THE ARCHAEOLOGICAL RECORD

There is strong and cogent archaeological evidence that communities living in Iron Age and Roman-period Britain and Europe nurtured beliefs concerning the dead and the afterlife. Indeed, classical writers such as Pomponius Mela and Diodorus Siculus make it clear that people in ancient Gaul believed in some form of reincarnation, and an embodied eternity in the otherworld. But there is an ambivalence surrounding the interpretations of these Graeco-Roman chroniclers of ancient Gallo-British belief-systems concerning immortality. For them, reincarnation meant one of two things: either a dead person was reborn in the same physical body as before, or life after death involved occupying a new body, time after time, for eternity.

The archaeological evidence for the disposal of the dead supports the notion that in Iron Age and Roman Britain and Gaul (as elsewhere in Europe), communities believed in some form of afterlife. While by no means everyone received formal burial rites, those that did appear to reflect the notion of some kind of belief in immortality, via the placement in tombs of goods, precious possessions and even food, drink and feasting equipment. Excavation of the great burial mound belonging to a chief at Hochdorf in Germany, who died in the sixth century BC, revealed a dinner service for nine guests and a huge cauldron that had once contained mead. This is one of many such princely tombs in the region. Much closer to home and – for me at any rate – far more poignant is a grave for a baby boy who died of hydrocephalus in Roman Britain when he was less than a year old. His tomb was found in 1990 at Arrington in

Cambridgeshire. Small children appear to have only rarely been given formal burials but this one was different. His body was placed in a lead coffin, wrapped in multi-coloured woollen fabric, and there was evidence that his funeral involved the burning of incense imported from the Near East, suggesting that perhaps the child came from a cosmopolitan family. Most telling, though, is the collection of small white clay figurines that were buried with him, that date his death to the later first or early- to mid-second century AD. The little figures included sheep, two busts of smiling children and, most significantly, a mother-goddess. The goddess wore a distinctive 'beehive' headdress (or hairstyle), which is typical of Rhenish depictions of these deities, supporting the notion of this family's foreign connections. The goddess figurine from the Arrington grave sits in a high-backed chair, wearing flowing robes and holding a basket of fruit in her lap. Might it be that she was placed there as a comfort and protection to the little boy and, perhaps, to guide him safely to the otherworld? Her basket of food may have been interred with the baby to nourish him on his journey. With her by his side, there was perhaps no need to bury food and drink with his body.

Dreams and otherworlds: the tale of Macsen Wledig

One of the eleven tales in the group of mythic stories that make up the *Mabinogion* is 'The Dream of the Emperor Macsen'. The term *wledig* means 'lord'. Macsen has been identified as Magnus Maximus, who commanded the Roman army in Britannia in the late fourth century AD, and whose troops proclaimed him Emperor of Rome in AD 383. The tale of his dream begins with a hunting expedition that starts in Rome. This echoes the story of Pwyll and Arawn (in the First Branch) and that of Manawydan and Pryderi (in the Third Branch) and shows that hunting is a storytelling trope or theme used to herald a supernatural happening or an encounter with the otherworld. Woods and forests are common features in fairy tales (such as 'Hansel and Gretel' and 'Little Red Riding Hood'). Woodlands are sources of wonder and danger in J. R. R. Tolkien's *The Hobbit* and *The Lord of the Rings*. And so it may have been in this tale too. It is as if the hunt provided a bridge between worlds and that link might have been charged either with menace or an opportunity for good. The sun was high in the sky and Macsen grew tired on this hunting expedition and ordered the party to stop so he could sleep by the side of a river. And he had a dream.

The visions that Macsen saw while dreaming seem steeped in magic. He sees a great hall set out for feasting, with a golden floor and golden couches. There are beautiful women – particularly one maiden, with whom he falls in love – and handsome lads, all decked out in brocaded silk and fine jewels. When Macsen was woken from his dream, without the beautiful maiden he was now enamoured of, it was as if he had had to turn his back on the wondrous otherworld he had witnessed and return to a grey world of reality. Indeed, the emperor became so obsessed with what he had seen in his dream that he urged his men to go out and search for the magical world he had lost. His followers tracked down this world to Britannia, sailing over the sea to north Wales and coming, at last, to Aber Saint (around Caernarfon) and its castle. Inside was the great hall that Macsen had seen in his dream, and the maiden with whom he had fallen in love. They reported back to the emperor, travelling night and day until they arrived in Rome, and the emperor immediately set out with them back to Britain to claim the maiden as his empress. After seven years of wedded bliss with his Welsh bride, Macsen left Britain for Rome, conquering France as he went. But because he had been away for so long, the Romans had elected another emperor in his place. Eventually, Macsen reclaimed his empire.

Was his sojourn in Britain a reality or a dream? Was the story woven around Britannia because it was clothed in the mystery of distance? For this storyteller – who might have been a foreigner and used to more clement weather in his own homeland – did the stormy, foggy land of Britannia perhaps represent the otherworld? Remember the mist that overcame Dyfed when Manawydan's land was spellbound. Mists cloud sight and can therefore be perceived as spooky, full of ghostly presences and – for the susceptible imagination – suggesting otherworldliness.

Mirror-imaging and world wars

The Sámi people of Arctic Europe believed (and some may still do so) that the dead lived in a mirror world beneath that of earthly humans, and walked upside down in the footsteps of the living. Presumably, such foot-to-foot contact enabled the dead to have sufficient engagement with the living that they could siphon off enough energy to move their inert bodies. It would appear that the Sámi otherworld (or their 'land of the dead') involved 'mirror-imaging', with an invisible boundary between the living and the dead, sealing an inverted underworld or otherworld. This might strike a chord with readers familiar with the Netflix series *Stranger Things*, with its parallel yet topsy-turvy universe. For the Sámi, we can imagine a horizontal barrier separating the two worlds, one above the other. But in Welsh mythic tradition, the two realms were perceived to be in a parallel and linear relationship with one another. For example, Pwyll could step with ease (with Arawn's blessing) over the threshold that brought him into Annwfn.

The notion of mirror-imaging leads me to consider the symbolism of water. With its capacity, when still, to reflect accurately the world above it, water is just like a mirror. And so it would not be such a huge leap of faith to believe in stretches of water as the liminal or marginal space between near-identical worlds – those of the living people and of the spirits and/or the dead. Perceptions such as these may well have triggered the ancient custom (traceable archaeologically throughout the Bronze and Iron Ages) in much of northern and western Europe of casting weapons, other valued objects and even people into water or marshes, perhaps to appease the spirits thought to dwell beneath the boundary-layer of water. It is difficult not to bring to mind the tale of King Arthur's acquisition of Excalibur from the sacred lake and the need for it to be returned to its rightful magical domain as he lay dying. Many Welsh (and Irish) myths contain persistent reference to water: whether lakes, pools, rivers or the sea. Fords and bridges feature prominently in the Welsh storytelling tradition. The ability of Brân to use his body as a bridge over a great river, and to stride through the sea from north Wales to Ireland and cross those boundaries, perhaps serves to endorse the idea that this hero had an otherworldly dimension.

The idea of freeze-framing a transformation, in this case between life and death, is also evident in the Welsh tales. In the Fourth Branch, Lleu's murder, at the hands of his faithless flower-wife Blodeuwedd and her lover, resulted not in the victim's death but in his transformation. Lleu's eagle-body begins to decay, while he is still living. This is reminiscent of traditions of excarnation, where dead bodies were left exposed in high places so that the flesh could be picked clean by scavenging birds, thus allowing the liberation of the dead person's soul. Lleu was caught in stasis, in a 'between place', neither in this living earthly world nor in the hereafter.

Brân's half-brothers Nisien and Efnisien are presented as two opposites, representing good and evil or the hero and the anti-hero. However, their very names suggest mirror-imaging and the positive and negative facets of paired individuals. The oppositional imaging found on the plaque in the grave at Bad Dürkheim presented contradictory depictions of young/old and female/male. In a way, Brân's brothers reflect something similar: two halves of a whole, or two sides of the same coin. Perhaps the author of the tale was endeavouring to project the notion that Nisien and Efnisien represented a single entity, encompassing the dark and light aspects that exist – sometimes in conflict – within each of us. Nisien walked in the light and sunny uplands of the world while Efnisien's world was dark and twisted. Despite the total opposition of their characters, they were, in a sense, essential one to the other in that they could not exist without their opposite. Just as day and night share the mutual existence of opposition, so do good and evil: the one cannot exist without the other. In the Biblical narrative of Christ's Passion and death, Judas was necessary for Jesus to fulfil his destiny. So, perhaps, Efnisien also had a crucial

MIRROR-IMAGING
IN ANCIENT ICONOGRAPHY

A very specific group of decorated metal objects dating from Iron Age Britain and Europe points to the belief in oppositional or binary worlds, perhaps representative of the world of living humans and that of the spirits and/ or the dead. One fascinating example from Germany, dating to the earlier Iron Age (circa late fifth–early fourth century BC), is a tiny plaque made from sheet gold, from the tomb of a woman found at Bad Dürkheim, in the form of a human face. Turned one way up, it depicts the face of an elderly, bearded man, with bags beneath his eyes and a furrowed brow; turned upside down, though, the face is that of a smiling young girl, with her hair piled on top of her head. So, maybe, what is being conveyed here is the juxtaposition and contradiction, not only of age and gender, but also the opposed worlds of the living and the dead. Another artefact, a late Iron Age find that was made in the first century BC, was found in the English Cotswolds. It consists of a copper-alloy horse-harness mount decorated in red and blue enamel. The main image displayed on this piece is a pair of mirror-imaged owls' faces, one the right way up, the other upside down, depending on which way it is viewed. It is tempting to interpret it as having relevance to the myth of Blodeuwedd, though that is probably purely fanciful. Of course, this motif might have been purely for decoration, yet it is possible that, like so much military Iron Age art, it contained a symbolic message, associated with warfare and the predatory skill of owls. However, at a deeper level, could it have contained an allegorical message concerning ideas of mortality, darkness and the conundrum of death?

part to play in his eventual rescue of Brân's depleted forces by breaking apart the cauldron and thus robbing it of its power to resurrect Irish soldiers killed in the battle. In doing so, Efnisien redeemed himself and, as a result, had a much more muscular part to play in the war between Wales and Ireland than his brother.

Ancestral domains?

The apparent conundrum between an otherworld, as described in the First Branch of the *Mabinogion*, and an underworld of the dead might be resolved, in part at any rate, by acknowledgement of the role played by ancestors in many traditional societies, both past and ongoing. The Welsh myths contain no specific references to ancestors and what became of them or their souls. Yet, of course, there is a veiled allusion to the after-dead in the episode in the Second Branch, where Matholwch's slain warriors were reborn after being immersed in the magic cauldron of regeneration. These revivified men were not restored fully whole: the storyteller emphasised that they belong to the dead by their inability to access all five of their senses, for they cannot speak. And perhaps it is relevant to refer to Arawn's faculties as lord of Annwfn, which did not include his power to fight and repel his rival Hafgan. So, might we read into these patchy references the idea of continued existence in some form, but lacking certain aspects of humanity? And were the ancestral dead a pale copy of their flesh-girt lives? It is possible to imagine that, if ancestors of the mythic-dead were to inhabit another world, only those who had lived a good life would be allowed to join the throng of ancestor-spirits, whose job it might be to look after their living relatives. So characters such as Brân, Nisien and Rhiannon would be granted entry but the evil ones, such as Efnisien and Blodeuwedd, would find the gate firmly closed. However, it is worth wondering whether Efnisien's final act might have served to redeem his evil-doing and have, perhaps, allowed him to enter paradise.

Water-worlds as 'other'

The idea of water as a liminal place and gateway to the otherworld, that we explored in the mention of mirror-imaging, is very widespread in certain traditions. For instance, in communities associated with shamanism, river confluences and rapids are imagined as sacred crossing places where the realms of humans and spirits veered particularly close to one another. In Roman Gaul, at the confluence of the two great rivers, the Rhône and Saône, at Condate, just outside Lugdunum (Lyon), a great cult-centre was founded to acknowledge the sacred power of the rivers meeting. So important did it seem, even to the occupying Romans, that a temple to the Roman Imperial Cult was built to honour the emperor Augustus, founded on 1 August, 12 BC. Despite its *romanitas*, it was a Gaulish priest, from the tribe of the Aedui, who presided over its ritual events. It is highly significant, too, that the date of the temple's foundation coincided with the great Gallo-British-Irish festival of Lughnasadh (in August).

Confluences of water can be turbulent, like rapids in shallow, fast-flowing rivers and waterfalls. In societies associated with shamanism, such energy and the connections either between bodies of water (as in confluences) or between water and land (as in rapids) may easily be interpreted as specially charged and, sometimes, as a sign of spiritual presence.

The notion of sacred water is relevant to the Welsh mythic narratives as a gateway to the otherworld, as we have already explored. But there is another point of significance to the stories: the role of cauldrons. I wonder whether such great vessels, designed to hold huge quantities of liquid, may have been perceived as the otherworld in microcosm. Furthermore, the liquid inside a cauldron was often boiling and in a state of flux and movement which would mean that it was charged with the same spiritual imagery as rapids or a confluence of water. This makes sense in terms of Brân's cauldron of rebirth and regeneration. There is a power held within cauldrons. Readers might recall the popular series of fictional comic books set in ancient Gaul featuring Asterix, where his strongman sidekick Obelix was granted invincible strength by having fallen into the druid Getafix's cauldron containing a magic potion.

DOUBLE WORLDS: WATER AND PAIRING
IN MATERIAL CULTURE

It is notable that, in Iron Age Britain and Europe, there appears to have been a persistent tradition of placing paired objects in water, probably as sacrificial acts. And it is possible that this practice might represent an acknowledgement of water as an interface between the human world and the other-world. Cauldrons were one such object, and another recurrent pairing is that of spoons. Furthermore, these were not just everyday objects for food preparation but were made and used for specifically ritual purposes. The spoons are notable in their design. The bowl of one spoon is divided into quadrants, and a hole is drilled into the other one. These spoons are otherwise plain, except for their handles, which are heavily decorated with highly symbolic La Tène (European Iron Age) motifs, often in the form of S-shaped scrolls and curly-armed triskeles or triskelions (three-armed 'whirligig' designs), as if to transfer sanctity and spiritual power to the person holding them.

The spoons only 'work' in any practical sense if they are used together. Recent experiments with copies made for the British Museum found that if the spoons are placed together, with their convex surfaces facing outwards, powder made from bone-dust, dried blood, ochre or some other dry or liquid substance could be blown through the hole in the upper spoon, using some kind of straw, perhaps made from a hollow bird-bone, and the pattern of spatter that fell on the inner, quartered surface of the lower spoon might be interpreted to determine the will of the gods. Most of these paired spoons, like the cauldrons, come from watery or boggy places.

More pairing is evident in certain Iron Age bog bodies from northern and western Europe. At Weerdinge in the

Netherlands, two young men were interred together, apparently embracing. Both were sunk into the mire naked and both had been violently killed. They died towards the end of the Iron Age, between the second century BC and the late first century AD. Why pair 'sacrificed' people in this manner? Could it be that, like paired cauldrons and spoons, such an act spoke to both the worlds of the living and the dead? The placing of bodies in bogs was itself an acknowledgement of duality, because interring bodies in this manner prevents them from decaying at a normal rate and so they might be perceived, therefore, as being frozen inbetween states rather than the flesh being allowed to fall away and release the soul to join the ancestral spirits.

There is a broader dimension, too, in the backstory of Brân's cauldron. When Brân offered the Irish king his precious vessel, he expressed his surprise that the Irish king had not heard of it, as it had originally come from Ireland. Matholwch corrected him and said that he did, indeed, know of the cauldron and he then told Brân its story. He said that his first glimpse of it was as it was being borne out of a lake (the Lake of the Cauldron) when he was out hunting (another strange event associated with hunting). Not only was Matholwch hunting but he was also on top of a mound when he saw the vessel (as Pwyll was when he first saw Rhiannon). We will explore more about the significance of cauldrons in Chapter 5.

'Thisness' and 'thereness': ideas of the other

In his riveting second autobiographical book, *A Mad World, My Masters: Tales from a Traveller's Life*, John Simpson laments the sameness that has flattened out differences between various parts of Britain, Europe and the world. Time was, he writes with regret, when 'foreign' meant strange, weird and exciting, but by the twenty-first century, it has become increasingly difficult to find places which are totally outside one's experience or knowledge. So, to use his terminology, 'thisness' has blotted or ironed out 'thereness' or 'otherness'. Airports, cities and hotels worldwide possess a sad uniformity, and travellers sometimes look in vain for the outlandish or the challenge of newness. Only a very few areas of the wild world remain unexplored and much of it has been tamed by roads, rail networks and the speed and ease of air travel. So the world has lost something precious: many of the differences between communities, nationalities and, to an extent, environments.

IMAGING REBIRTH

In May 1891, peat cutters in the Danish Raevemose bog unearthed a spectacular find: a great, gilded, silver cauldron, known to us as the Gundestrup cauldron. It had been carefully dismantled into its thirteen constituent plates, and placed on a small dry island in the middle of the bog, perhaps a deliberate act to signify that it belonged to both dry and wet worlds – or those of earthly beings and the spirits of the dead. Each plate was covered in images, worked in repoussé. As well as the woman having her hair braided that we looked at in Chapter 3, there are more complex images engraved on the cauldron. Perhaps the most striking of them is the iconography of one of its inner, narrative panels, which apparently depicts a resurrection scene very similar to that chronicled in the Second Branch of the *Mabinogion*. This war-scene has two registers, divided horizontally by a fallen tree. In the lower tier, a line of foot soldiers marches towards a supernaturally large 'human' figure who is in the act of dipping each upside-down warrior into a bucket or cauldron. The upper register displays another line of soldiers, this time on horseback, riding away from the super-sized figure and the cauldron. It is so very tempting to perceive this tableau as representative of a scene of Brân's cauldron of regeneration. The cauldron was probably made and used in the very late Iron Age (circa first century BC). While there is no direct link between the iconography on an early artefact found in a remote location in Denmark and Welsh mythic tales, the similarity between the image on the Gundestrup cauldron and the story of Brân's is striking and unexplained. What the similarity between the motif on the Gundestrup cauldron and the Welsh mythic tale certainly reinforces is the idea that shared sacred stories may have been circulated and retold over hundreds of years by myth-spinners and that they probably travelled widely within Britain and beyond.

To the people who told the Welsh myths, first orally and then in written form, to Welsh audiences and then readers, it was the otherworld that held 'thereness' or strangeness. This may explain why dreams – such as those of Rhonabwy and Macsen – played such a prominent role in the collection of enchantment tales that make up the *Mabinogion* alongside the Branches. Dreams are peculiar phenomena. It is in dreams that one can encounter weird and untracked places, be faced with sometimes dangerous and inexplicable situations, and come face to face with the living entities of the long-dead. Dreamscapes, which are highly individual because they emanate from our never-sleeping brains, allow the sleeper to travel through time and space without stirring from their bed. And often, when awakened, the dreamer cannot even remember the elusive experience of the night. So the brain while dreaming is a gateway to a 'thereness' which can be visited only when the boundary between waking and sleeping has been breached. I have been told that, if a person's sight deteriorates dramatically and swiftly, they may become subject to hallucinations, and see powerful images of people, places or things that they cannot explain. According to the science, this happens because the brain, starved of visual stimuli, compensates by inventing its own images to fill the void. So, in a sense, people having these visions are entering a variation of dream-world.

In some senses, it is plausible to view so much of the Welsh mythic narrative in terms of 'otherness' and otherworldliness, yet clothed in a 'cloud of unknowing', to quote an anonymous fourteenth-century work (called by this name) of Christian mysticism. Sometimes the cloud clears in the narrative to shine a light on the Welsh otherworld. It is explicitly revealed in the tale of Pwyll and Arawn as adjacent to the human world, though better, brighter and more sumptuous, if less stable. It is like Matholwch's dead warriors when they emerge from Brân's magic cauldron. These slain soldiers had made the journey to the realms of the dead and returned, resurrected, to fight again as living men. But they bore the 'mark of Cain' inasmuch as their dumbness signified their sojourn in the otherworld. The fact that they had left their speech behind indicated that they still belonged to Annwfn. What about Rhiannon's strange appearance to Pwyll, as he sat on his sacred mound? Was the *Gorsedd* a 'between' place, a corridor where the two worlds met? And was that what enabled Rhiannon to cross the divide? And did her unbeatable horse again signify that both she and her mount had an otherworldly dimension? What of the mist that suddenly descended upon Manawydan, Rhiannon, Pryderi and Cigfa when the occupants of the land of Dyfed were put under an evil spell and vanished: were those lost people and animals taken to the otherworld, only to be returned to earth when the curse was lifted? The more the surface of the mythic narrative is scratched, the more it reveals, not in so many words (except occasionally), but repeatedly referred to, albeit obliquely. And medieval listeners and readers would have learnt to navigate the stories and to guess when this veiled world showed itself.

CHAPTER 5

Capricious Cauldrons and Burnished Bowls

*'I was hunting in Ireland one day, on top of a mound
overlooking a lake that was in Ireland, and it was called
the Lake of the Cauldron. And I beheld a big man with
yellow-red hair coming from the lake with a cauldron on his
back. Moreover he was a monstrous man, big and the evil
look of a brigand about him, and a woman following after
him. And if he was big, twice as big as he was the woman.'*

This quotation is from the Second Branch of the *Mabinogion* and is
the words of Matholwch explaining his first sighting of the cauldron
that Brân has presented to him as a reparation-gift after his brother
Efnisien's mutilation of the king's horses. Matholwch was mollified
(at least at first) by Brân's gesture. Before this, Brân explained that he
had received the vessel from a man who had acquired it in Ireland,
but he had no idea where this person had got it. Matholwch was able
to impart his own knowledge of the cauldron's genesis which began
when he witnessed its emergence from an Irish lake – the Lake of the
Cauldron. Readers may be struck by a nugget of significance from
this opening quote, namely, Matholwch's witnessing of the cauldron's

81

Efnisien destroys Brân's cauldron,
bursting his own heart as he does so.

appearance while he was situated on a mound, the same as Pwyll when he had the first magical vision of Rhiannon on her horse in the First Branch. Was this repetition of the image of the mound a message to the storyteller's audience, to flag up that something peculiar and special was about to happen?

Matholwch's bizarre narrative continued with the description of the two huge and monstrous people who bore the cauldron to the shore of the lake. As they emerged, the couple exchanged greetings with the king, and the man explained the strangeness of his companion or 'wife' (if that was indeed who she was). She, he said, conceived one son every six weeks and then gave birth to a fully armed warrior. She now had several sons. Astounded by this account, Matholwch decided to take the couple and their boys home with him but, in his kingdom, they became more and more obstreperous and harmful to his people, so much so that they threatened to unseat him from his kingship. Forced to do something to rid his land of this dreadful pair and the woman's offspring, the king agreed with his council that they must be annihilated. So it was decided to summon every smith from all over Ireland to construct an iron house, and then surround it with charcoal. Then they lured the man, the woman and her sons into the iron house and plied them with a huge feast and liquor until they were all blind drunk and comatose. Then they lit the charcoal until the iron house was white-hot. The warrior-children perished but the man and the woman survived. The pair then escaped to Wales and that was how Brân acquired his magic cauldron of rebirth. Cauldrons in Irish myth were capricious and characterful. Could it be that the cauldron that emerged from the Irish lake made its own decision to return to the land of its 'birth' after its sojourn in Wales?

Another Irish cauldron appears in the Welsh mythic tales. In 'Culhwch and Olwen', the capture of another Irish cauldron, the 'cauldron of Diwrnach', was one of the impossible tasks demanded of Culhwch and Arthur by Ysbaddaden. The giant was sufficiently confident of the heroes' impending failure to acquire it that he teased them by joking that the cauldron would be handy for boiling meat for Culhwch and Olwen's wedding feast. Arthur led the raid on Ireland where he killed the cauldron's owner, Diwrnach, and sailed back to Wales with it, packed with all the treasures of Ireland. Arthur and his precious cargo disembarked at Porth Cerddin near Fishguard, which was renamed Mesur-y-Peir (the 'Measure of the Cauldron').

Cauldrons and bowls: the significance of vessels

Cauldrons are special and freighted with meaning. Cauldrons are often presented as objects of evil. Shakespeare's powerful image of the three witches from *Macbeth*, huddled around their cauldron, brewing noxious substances from unspeakable ingredients and whispering curses, springs to mind.

The ancient Greek chronicler Strabo, writing in the first century BC, describes a horrific custom among the Cimbri tribe who occupied the region of Schleswig-Holstein in the far north of Germany and southern Denmark. Strabo speaks of the hideous execution of prisoners of war by ancient priestesses dressed in white, who placed decorative crowns upon victims, bound their hands, and then led them up to a great bronze cauldron mounted on a step. Each prisoner was made to kneel with his head hanging over the rim of the vessel; then his throat was cut with a slash of a sword by one of the old women, and the blood spilled into the cauldron. Afterwards, the priestesses cut open their victims' bodies and, from examination of their innards, they believed they would be able to tell the future and secure victory for their people.

In medieval times, cauldrons had a clear primary use: to hold large amounts of liquid and for cooking communal meals, such as boiled meat. So they probably played a prominent role in hospitality, the sharing of food with immediate and more distant family members, with friends, neighbours, guests and allies. They would have been expensive to make – and also to buy – usually being fashioned out of beaten bronze. In the tenth century AD, Hywel Dda (Hywel the Good) ruled much of Wales. He is remembered mostly for his law-making. These laws were codified in the thirteenth century, and they are interesting in this context because they established cauldrons as prestige goods. The laws state that a 'goodman' should have three indispensable possessions:

a harp, a cloak and a cauldron. A cauldron was identified as a standard piece of kit for a nobleman. More interesting still is that, although they were essentially cooking vessels, they were perceived as belonging to men rather than women, should it be necessary (as in the case of divorce) to apportion goods between marriage partners.

The codification of Hywel Dda's laws is broadly contemporary with the writing-down of the Welsh myths, and so it makes sense for cauldrons to figure so prominently in some of the stories. But how did it come about that they assumed supernatural status? Did it happen simply because they were transformative objects, having the ability to turn raw ingredients into palatable food and drink? Or was it something to do with 'commensality', the communal meal? This would have been important in the forging of friendships and alliances and, of course, storytelling would have taken place around the hearth.

The cauldrons of Welsh myth appear to have a light and a dark side to them. Brân's cauldron could be a force for good, in its regenerative role, but it could also turn on its keeper. The 'evil' facet might refer back to the remote, Iron Age, past when, if Strabo is to be believed, cauldrons were used as ritual utensils to catch the blood of human sacrificial victims.

And what of the golden bowl that snared Rhiannon and Pryderi in the Third Branch? This vessel was 'tricky' too. It was charged with a 'fixing' spell, meaning that any human that touched it would immediately be rooted to the spot, and would not be released from its grip until its magic was undone by the spellcaster. The importance of the scene rests upon touch, the connection between the bowl's outer surface and the skin of whoever laid hands on it. The storyteller does not go into any details as to the bowl's size or whether it was decorated, or filled with liquid. We know that the bowl was 'golden'. It may not have been made of pure gold but possibly gilded or even just highly polished bronze. Its magic may, indeed, be associated with its shine. In some traditional communities, 'shimmer' carries significance, partly because of the reflective properties of shiny things but also partly because shimmering involves movement – the oscillation of light on a surface that can make objects appear as iridescent and radiate many colours. The curved surfaces of bowls (and cauldrons) would enhance such shimmer. And the contents of vessels such as these may also have reflective properties, whether water, wine, oil or blood: all would have gleamed in sunlight or firelight.

FIXING CURSES

The binding properties of the golden bowl that trapped Rhiannon and Pryderi call to mind a much earlier 'fixing' ritual, though there is absolutely no evidence of a direct connection, as we saw in Chapter 2. During the Iron Age and Roman periods in Britain and Europe (including Wales), there was a custom whereby people who felt aggrieved by another's actions would take a small piece of beaten lead or pewter and scrawl a curse on the soft metal surface (or ask a scribe to do it for them). These were ritual acts and they appealed to the gods for retribution against those who had done them wrong – harm that was usually associated with theft (whether it be money, a pair of boots, a ring or a girlfriend). What is significant about these messages to the spirits is the punishment that was requested – sometimes demanded – of the gods: it was brutal and extreme, and usually involved bodily functions associated with blood, the inability to pass water or to have sex, and various other dire threats. Some of these plaques bear nail-holes where they had been fixed to gates or wooden walls. Others were rolled up because of the perceived need for the curse to be secret and only for divine eyes. At Roman Bath, many curses directed for the attention of the presiding goddess, Sulis Minerva, were not only folded up but cast into the sacred water, thought to embody Sulis herself.

Cauldrons with attitude

Preiddeu Annwfn (*The Spoils of Annwfn*) and the story of Ceridwen's cauldron from 'The Tale of Taliesin' belong, in their written forms, to the earliest and latest medieval period respectively. The poem, *Preiddeu Annwfn* may have been written down as early as AD 900, while 'The Tale of Taliesin' in written form might date from as late as the sixteenth century. The central character in both these tales is a cauldron with 'attitude': a vessel not only with a mind of its own but with a habit of tricking people. In *The Spoils of Annwfn*, Arthur was once again involved in cauldron-rustling, travelling down to the otherworld to steal lord Arawn's cauldron. This vessel is described as gleaming with the precious stones that adorned its surface, so it was a prize indeed. (In researching the archaeological evidence for Welsh Iron Age cauldrons, I have pondered on the nature of their manufacture, noting that the many bronze rivets used – like those on the vessels in the hoard excavated at Llyn Fawr – would have shone with faceted brilliance when new, almost like diamonds). But this underworld cauldron was also full of magic and mischief. It was choosy in allowing itself to be used for boiling liquid, and demanded the breath of nine virgins to heat it (presumably to reflect the undissipated sexual energy of maidenhood, similar to that ascribed to Goewin, Math's foot-holder in the Fourth Branch of the *Mabinogi*). And this cauldron also had the power to choose for whom it would cook food: only for the brave and honourable and not for cowards. And there was a sting in the tail for the thief that stole it from its rightful place in the otherworld. Nearly all Arthur's raiding party came to grief. While three boatloads of warriors went with Arthur to capture this vessel, only seven of his fighters came home. It is clear from this tale that Annwfn's cauldron was steeped in the danger that pervaded the otherworld and radiated harm to living humans who dared cross its threshold unbidden.

Ceridwen was a witch, and witches possessed cauldrons in which they brewed mixtures containing magic spells. Ceridwen's cauldron is endowed with the status of a living thing and given powerful agency. It could make choices, rather like the otherworld cauldron that Arthur stole. Ceridwen's cauldron could be seen to defy her wishes and bestow her gift of wisdom on the young boy, Gwion, rather than to Afagddu, the ill-favoured one. Her cauldron is just one of many weird and wonderful things in Welsh myths that crossed boundaries of reality and possessed abilities that – in the real world – were denied to all but living creatures.

Not surprisingly, given their use, there is a close connection between these vessels and water (or other liquids) in Welsh (and also Irish) mythic narratives. Brân's cauldron appears to have been borne from an Irish lake, and made the voyage across the Irish Sea to Wales and back. Likewise, the cauldron of Diwrnach, plundered by Arthur, made the sea journey from Ireland to west Wales. The lovely illustration of this vessel, brimming with Irish treasures, in Gwyn and Thomas Jones's elegant translation of the tale (published by Dent in 1976) shows the cauldron being floated across the sea together with one of the raiding boats, almost like a ship itself. The boiling of sacred liquid in these great, spiritually charged vessels had the power to resurrect the dead and empower people with great knowledge. Such powers were also given to the Salmon of Llyn Llyw, encountered in Culhwch's quest for Olwen, which once again exhibits a link between wisdom and the sea.

In early medieval Irish mythology, there is a tale that chimes strongly with Brân's cauldron of regeneration. One of the Irish gods, the craftsman/physician Dian Cécht, had the ability to restore dead warriors to life by immersing them in a well, while chanting spells. And scattered about the Insular (Irish) mythic tales are references to the recycling of human heads for use as sacred, life-restoring drinking cups. This theme is picked up in Welsh hagiography, where Saint Teilo's skull, perceived as a holy relic containing the saint's essence, was fashioned into a cup from which the sick could drink healing water from a holy well.

Efnisien and the bursting cauldron

There is an interesting facet to the ultimate fate of Brân's cauldron and it is one that is opaquely referenced in the ancient cauldrons discovered at various archaeological sites. We are already familiar with the waywardness of this cauldron and its fellows. This cauldron turns on its previous owner by regenerating the slain warriors of Brân's enemy,

Matholwch. It is during this battle that Brân's malevolent half-brother, Efnisien, redeemed himself for his act that began the Welsh–Irish war by jumping into the cauldron – destroying both himself and the vessel. The storyteller narrates the bursting of Efnisien's heart at the same moment as the cauldron itself, and I think meant the audience to identify the cauldron with its destroyer. And what about the cauldron's obliteration? Does it tell us something about the nature of its construction? We can refer to the make-up of Iron Age cauldrons such as those found at Llyn Fawr. They were made of thin bronze sheets joined together with numerous rivets. It was, therefore, an easier thing to break up than would be the case with a single piece of cast or beaten metal. I am convinced that some of these Welsh mythic tales were built upon much earlier traditions and may even have been influenced by witnessing fragments of ancient vessels that might occasionally have been seen at the edges of lakes and pools, particularly when water levels dropped during droughts. This idea might seem fanciful perhaps, but not impossible. And even if such a theory can be dismissed, it should be noted that, although the way they were manufactured changed over time, their use continued into the medieval period, so myth-spinners would have been familiar with these large cooking vessels.

Prestige, feasting and sacrifice

The link between cauldrons and watery places has a further dimension: that of value or prestige. This is evident in a find from Duchcov in Bohemia (Czech Republic). Sometime in the third century BC, a huge cauldron was filled with jewellery before being deposited in a thermal spring. Such a find chimes with the Carlingwark cauldron which was stuffed with iron objects and then placed in a Scottish lake. The prestige element in cauldron-symbolism – both in archaeology and myth – relates not simply to the object itself but also to its contents, whether it is filled with perishable food items or valuable objects such as tools, weapons or jewels. Once again, we are reminded of Arthur's pillage of Diwrnach's great cauldron brimming with treasure.

Underpinning the prestige associated with cauldrons are two related

THE ARCHAEOLOGY OF CAULDRONS AND WATERY PLACES

The association between cauldrons (and other vessels) and water goes further than their basic function of holding liquids (water, liquor and even blood) and that is strongly reflected in Iron Age ritual symbolism. These vessels were frequently deposited in watery places: lakes, pools and swamps. It almost seems as though the cauldrons themselves symbolised enclosed bodies of water, such as pools, in microcosm.

In Wales, two highly relevant archaeological sites were found at Llyn Fawr in the south Wales valleys and Llyn Cerrig Bach on the island of Anglesey. Respectively, they bracket the beginning and end of the Welsh Iron Age. But, despite the long time gap between their origins (the hoard at Llyn Fawr dates to around 700 BC and Llyn Cerrig Bach to the second century BC/first century AD), the placements of two cauldrons at both watery sites bear striking similarities. Perhaps the most significant is that of pairing. Why deposit two of these precious vessels? Was it because of a belief in dual upper and lower worlds? If these cauldrons and their contents were votive gifts – as I am sure they were – were they doubled in order to reflect attempts at appeasement of the spirits perceived to dwell in both domains? Perhaps they represented offerings to the ancestral dead (below) and the gods (in the upper realms of the cosmos). I find it fascinating that cauldron-symbolism, particularly with its link to water, is as powerful in later prehistoric and earlier Roman Wales as in the context of the Welsh myths. But ancient Iron Age cauldron-pairing was not confined to Wales but also occurred in Scotland. At Blackburn Mill, a pair of cauldrons was found deposited in a bog, one carefully placed inside the other. A cauldron found in Carlingwark Loch was filled with iron objects and deposited in a lake. Although this cauldron's contents consisted of broken pieces, they would still have been considered recyclable and therefore valuable. Might it be that the brokenness of this ironwork possessed particular significance because it represented separation from the living world, making it appropriate for divine acceptance as a votive gift, especially by underworld spirits? The Carlingwark find, brimming with offerings, reminds me irresistibly of the cauldron of Diwrnach, stolen by Arthur and full of all of the treasures of Ireland.

themes: feasting and sacrifice. In ancient Greek rituals, the two concepts were closely associated. Cauldrons were used to cook meat, which was then divided into portions for the gods and for human consumption. The holiness of the meat offerings was inculcated not simply by means of prayers and incantations but also by the very act of boiling them in the cauldrons. For the Greeks, separate cauldrons were required for cooking and for sacrificial blood collection. Greek vases frequently feature paintings of animal sacrifice where a cauldron, called a *sphageion*, was used for the sole purpose of catching and containing the blood of the sacrificial victim whose throat was cut over the vessel. This custom recalls the Cimbrian execution rite chronicled by Strabo. We should bear in mind the likelihood that at least some of the medieval Welsh (and Irish) mythmakers, particularly the monks who wrote down the stories, would have had access to Greek and Roman texts, and have been influenced by them in their storytelling.

Ambivalence in meaning surrounds the significance of cauldrons. They were both life givers (food providers) and death vessels (blood

COMMUNAL DRINKING
AND ARCHAEOLOGY:
TANKARDS AND WINE VESSELS

The practice of communal feasting so evocatively represented by cauldrons is displayed in the archaeology of late Iron
Age vessels for communal drinking. A splendid example
is the beautiful tankard from Trawsfynydd in Gwynedd
(which now, alas, resides in a Liverpool museum, rather
than within its Welsh homeland). Like many cauldrons
– including those from Llyn Fawr and Llyn Cerrig Bach
– this vessel was found in a damp context, a mire. It was
constructed of yew wood and encased in sheet-bronze.
Like the pairs of spoons described in Chapter 4, the person
who made it played with the counterpoint of blankness
and decoration: the body of the tankard is totally plain
but the handle is a riot of curvilinear La Tène art. Its date
of manufacture was probably in the later first century AD,
and it might well have been placed in a sacred aquatic
place as part of a ritual to ask the gods to try and scupper
the Roman military presence in north Wales. The tankard
is large – the diameter of its rim more than eighteen
centimetres and its height is fourteen centimetres – and it
is clearly designed for sharing mead, ale or fermented berry
juice. It would have been passed round at feasts from guest
to guest. The very act of drinking from the same cup acted
as a symbol of alliances and comradeship. I suggest that the
decorative handle represented spiritual force; the changing
of hands as the tankard was passed perhaps acting as a
conduit for the sharing of the sacred (not dissimilar to the
shared chalice of the Christian Eucharist).

We can imagine that the feasts described in the Welsh myths included the exchange of alcohol in communal cups. Like the *symposia* of the ancient Greek tradition, such drinking customs perhaps involved strict etiquette – in terms of to whom the cup or tankard was offered first, and which way it would be passed around the feasting-board. These communal events would, of course, be accompanied by conversation or by entertainment such as music or storytelling. And perhaps prayers and libations to the spirits also played roles in dignifying and sanctifying the solemnity of high-level hospitality.

The notion of alcoholic drink as having a sacred dimension is given special credence by discoveries at late Iron Age *oppida* (fortified townships) in Gaul, where huge caches of Roman amphorae (large, two-handled pottery jars used for the containment and transport of wine in bulk) have been found. One of these sites, Corent in the Auvergne, yielded striking evidence for ritual wine consumption for, not only were these pottery wine jars hoarded, rather than being smashed and trashed, there is evidence that they were 'beheaded' by slicing through their necks with the cut of a sword. The shape of these amphorae bears an uncanny likeness to the human form: they are tall, they narrow at the top but are shaped as though they have shoulders, with their two handles resembling human arms. They would once have had lids and so they could have looked as if they had heads and long necks. Of course, their contents, too, would have contributed to this idea of humanity, because they would have held blood-red wine. Might these vessels have been ritually 'killed' while full of wine so that the 'blood' ran free, as surrogates for human sacrificial victims?

containers). Brân's cauldron oscillated between its ability to regenerate life – albeit of a kind – and the converse of destruction. Annwfn's cauldron tempted Arthur with its jewel-studded brightness but it also caused the virtual annihilation of his band of raiders. In a sense, both cauldrons were associated, albeit sometimes obliquely, with sacrifice. In order for there to be a gain, there had to be losses. If you wanted something from the gods, something else had to be sacrificed in order to propitiate or – to be cynical – to bribe the spirits. Reciprocity was crucial in the relationship between humans and the divine.

Another aspect of the link between cauldrons and the gods was feasting and commensality, whereby communities bonded through sharing food. In ancient Europe, communal eating was not just a method of social networking but fulfilled a much more important role in forging and cementing alliances, brokering marriages, settling disputes and engaging in commercial transactions. Hospitality played a pivotal part in social relationships, and there were intricate principles of etiquette involved. In the Welsh mythic tales, feasting is a recurrent theme, and we have already witnessed the chaos that could result from any breakage of the rules regarding the proper way of doing things. Efnisien's insult of Brân's royal Irish guest began a hideous sequence of events, leading ultimately to war and a huge loss of human life. In a sense, Brân's cauldron can be seen as a symbol of the carnage as it was the central character. We have to remember, too, that feasting not only means eating but also drinking, and quarrels as well as friendships can be fuelled by intoxication.

Cauldrons in archaeology and myth: connection or coincidence?

A famous late Iron Age silver-gilt cauldron was found at Gundestrup in Jutland, Denmark, a long way away from Wales. It is curiously connected to the Welsh myths, though.

The treatment and deposition of this vessel indicates the reverence with which it was regarded. Its iconography is enigmatic, bearing some elements that appear to belong to Gallic tradition, such as the images of deities, others that chime with northern European imagery and others again that speak of iconography hailing from further east. Its iconography is so rich and complex that it is appropriate to think of it as presenting a mythic narrative. The origin of the vessel is a puzzle for, during the late first century BC, when it was made, the production of large silver objects was almost entirely confined to Thrace in southeast Europe. So how can we reconstruct the journey this cauldron made from its possible place of manufacture to Denmark via Gaul? One theory, which may be fanciful but fits the facts, is that it was commissioned from Thracian silversmiths by Gaulish religious leaders (perhaps druids), delivered to Gaul and later looted by a raiding party of Cimbrian warriors and taken home to Denmark. There is literary evidence from classical authors that such raids took place. In Denmark, it was carefully taken apart (perhaps to neutralise its spiritual charge) and deposited as a ritual offering – in the remote spot, surrounded by water, where it was found many years later – possibly to a Germanic god of victory. However, and at the hands of whom, this multicultural cauldron ended up where it did, some aspects of its existence are clear. Whoever was responsible for depositing the cauldron took great trouble to dismantle its constituent plates and place them, one on top of the other, on a tiny dry island surrounded by bog.

Its imagery of gods, sacrificial acts and mythical scenes leaves no room for doubt about its ritual purpose. The inner surface of the cauldron's base plate is adorned with the image of a dying bull, its horns rearing up so that they look as if they would have pierced through the contents of the vessel (perhaps filled with the blood of the bovine sacrificial victim). There is also the imagery of a cauldron of regeneration echoing the story of Brân that we saw in Chapter 4. But, given the glaring discrepancies in time and place, how could the Gundestrup cauldron and the medieval mythic tale of Brân possibly be related? A definite answer will always elude us but, given the longevity of oral tradition in many societies around the world (a good example being the 12,000-year history of mythic storytelling among Aboriginal Australians), might early stories of rebirth have percolated down through the centuries and become woven into Welsh mythic tradition? It would only require one traveller to have returned from northern Europe, having seen the cauldron, or its fellows that are yet to be found or which didn't survive archaeologically, for the idea to be adopted into the rich palimpsest of storytelling. Whatever the whys and wherefores, there exists a striking likeness between the narrative of the Gundestrup cauldron and the magic cauldron of Brân. If such connective tissue cannot be confidently explained, it is nonetheless well worth pondering.

CHAPTER 6

Goddesses, Witches and Shamed Women

Peredur fell upon the witch and struck her on the head with his sword until her helm and headpiece spread like a salver on her head. 'Thy mercy, fair Peredur son of Efrawg, and the mercy of God!' [cried the witch]. 'How knowest thou, hag, that I am Peredur?' 'It was fated and foreseen that I should suffer affliction from thee, and that thou should take horse and arms from me. And thou shalt be with me awhile, being taught to ride thy horse and handle thy weapons.' 'On these terms', he replied, 'shalt thou have mercy: thy pledge that thou never do hurt to this countess's dominion.'

On his travels, the young eponymous hero of the *Mabinogion* tale, 'Peredur, son of Efrog', was on his travels when he came upon a castle set on a mountain top. He hammered on the door for entry and was met by a large, handsome young man and a Junoesque female figure, comely and surrounded by maidservants. Peredur requested that he be allowed to sleep in the castle that night. But the woman – a countess – demurred, explaining to the young nobleman that the castle and its inhabitants were being threatened by a plague of malevolent witches,

Blodeuwedd, 'Flower Face',
created by magicians Math and Gwydion.

the Nine Witches of Caer Loyw (Gloucester): so it was not safe for Peredur to stay. The woman explained that these awful women had already destroyed all her lands, apart from the castle itself. Peredur pledged to defend her and her household if trouble arose but said that he would not do harm to anyone.

When he awoke at daybreak, he heard a commotion. It was a witch challenging the watchman guarding the castle. So Peredur attacked her. Arthur had bonded with Peredur when the hero arrived at his court asking to be knighted; Arthur and his knights now joined Peredur to challenge the Nine Witches to battle, after the first witch that Peredur had encountered broke the vow he had asked her to swear, not to harm anyone close to Peredur. At this final skirmish, one of the witches fought Peredur and his companions, and was killed. As she died, she screamed a warning to her eight sisters to flee, yelling out to them the prophecy that the young hero was destined to destroy them all. And so it transpired. All the witches died at the hand of Peredur.

The strong links between Welsh and Irish mythology have already been cited throughout this book, particularly in the previous chapter that chronicles the Irish origin of Brân's cauldron and Arthur's purloining of another cauldron filled with treasure from Ireland. The Irish association in Peredur's tale is revealed in the first encounter between Peredur and one of the Nine Witches, where she offers to teach him warcraft. In the Ulster mythic tale, the '*Táin Bó Cuailnge*', the young champion Cú Chulainn underwent battle-training by a female tutor named Scáthach, her name having the sinister meaning 'She who walks in shadow'. Not only was Scáthach a formidable teacher of warcraft but also a seer and a prophet. In both her gender and her power to predict the future, she is described in virtually identical terms to Peredur's witch. Is this merely happenstance or does it reflect the sharing of stories across the Irish Sea?

Witches are generally portrayed as frightening. In human form they are often old and ugly and have powers of magic and connection with the dark spirits. *Macbeth*'s witches are a good example: hideous, terrifying and accurate in their prophecies. However, witchcraft is an obscure concept, and to define the term 'witch' is difficult. Witches in some form exist and have existed in the past all over the world. Some

PROPHETIC DRUIDESSES
AND JAWLESS SPELL-BINDERS

The theme of women as possessors of occult powers goes back a long way in ancient Britain and beyond. Classical literature (in a multi-author compilation of texts called the *Scriptores Historiae Augustae*, or *The Augustan Histories*) makes several references to the prophecies of religious women concerning the appointment of new emperors in the late Roman Empire. Diocletian, Numerian, Aurelian and Severus Alexander's reigns were all heralded by prophetic proclamations given by druidesses in Gaul. The story behind this is elusive but interesting. While male druids are frequently mentioned by a range of sources – from Julius Caesar in the mid first century BC to the poet and teacher Ausonius in the late fourth century AD – druidesses only appear in these late texts. Why did these holy women take centre stage now? It may be something to do with the perceived need for this clutch of late seekers of imperial power to be recognised not only among their own people, but even far away in foreign lands. And the switch from male to female druids in the texts may have been a storytelling trope designed to make accession to the 'imperial purple' (the emperorship of Rome and its empire) even more enigmatic and spiritually charged. The similarity between these obscure religious women and the witches of Welsh myth lies in their shared link with the otherworld which enabled them to see into the future.

There is some fascinating, if somewhat obscure, archaeological evidence for prophetic women in late Roman Britain. Several puzzling graves, found in Roman Winchester in Hampshire, and some others in Dorset, contained the bodies of middle-aged or elderly women with their heads cut off and placed by their knees or feet. Even more striking is that they sometimes had their lower jaws also removed from the rest of their heads. I wonder whether this indicates their possible status as mouthpieces for the spirits or, perhaps, as casters of spells who needed to be silenced, even in death. Speech is powerful. Even if these women had led blameless lives, the treatment of their bodies post-mortem displays a strange ritual process that may, just possibly, indicate a belief that they could wield witchcraft and had the ability to utter foul spells.

are benign, others malign. When witches crop up in Welsh mythology, they appear mainly as negative, malicious beings that pit their wits and magical powers for evil, and use their prophetic powers to meddle with people. However, this is not the case for all of them. Ceridwen is a witch but could she be defined as wholly malevolent? While vengeful to Gwion after he stole her son Afagddu's inheritance, it could be argued that her cauldron of wisdom-making stew was a force for good, leading ultimately to Gwion's rebirth as the shaman-poet Taliesin. But Peredur's witches are presented as utterly malign, drawing on dark spiritual powers to cause havoc in the world of humans. What is interesting about the tale of Peredur is that the Christian God is mentioned several times. In a sense, then, it might be permissible to think of the Nine Witches of Caer Loyw as symbols of the Antichrist or the Devil.

The 'calumniated wife'

There is very little feminism in Welsh (or Irish) myth. While male heroes strutted around the stories, rattling sabres and wielding power, females were given a more muted and often less sympathetic voice. Their sometimes 'divine' status may be hinted at but is always more veiled than that of the male characters. And many female figures – such as Rhiannon, Aranrhod and Blodeuwedd – are treated harshly by storytellers and, perhaps more particularly, by the scribes who wrote the tales down. Other female characters are undeveloped. Goewin, Math's foot-holder, for instance, could have played a fascinating role had her persona been fleshed out, yet all the storyteller cared about was her symbolism in relation to Math. Branwen should have been given a far more prominent part in the Second Branch of the *Mabinogion*. After all, it was she who actually triggered the catastrophic war between Wales and Ireland, firstly because of her betrothal to Matholwch, which was such anathema to her half-brother Efnisien, and secondly on account of her ill-treatment by her husband, which goaded Brân to take up arms against the Irish.

A strong thread running through all the Welsh myths is the attachment of blame to women and the punishments meted out to those who 'fall from grace'. Lurking behind some of this attitude to women might be the misogyny of those who wrote down the tales. These were, of course, Christian monks with their strict religious and ethical codes that, alas, not only saw women as subjugated to men, but tarred them with the same brush of blame as Eve in the Garden of Eden. Man reigned supreme over the earth but his inheritance from God was tainted because he had succumbed to female temptation.

This trope of woman-blaming sadly continues to this day. In my early youth I took a temporary job between leaving school and going to university, working for the excruciatingly named Council for the Unmarried Mother and her Child, where my aunt had a senior position. The title for this organisation was only just better than calling it the 'Council for Fallen Women'. Today's society is a little more enlightened but victims of sexual assault still encounter prejudicial questions by the police and by lawyers defending those accused of rape. These questions bring up their own blame as provocateurs of their assailants: perhaps they were walking alone at night, or wearing skimpy clothes – even though the only person responsible for the crime is the attacker.

Let us look in detail at the idea of blame and the female scapegoat in the Welsh myths. Two characters display the theme of the 'calumniated

RHIANNON
AND EPONA

In Roman Gaul and Britain – including Wales – a popular native horse-goddess was worshipped by devotees who erected inscribed dedications to her and invariably depicted her as a woman riding or accompanied by horses. Her name was Epona, from the Gaulish word *epos*, meaning 'horse'. Her importance is exhibited by her mention – unique for a Gallo-British divinity – in the Roman calendar that listed the festival days of prominent gods and goddesses in the Roman Empire. Among her devotees were cavalrymen in the Roman army, who looked to her to protect both them and their horses. And a more homely aspect to her cult is referenced by some of her imagery, which depicts the goddess seated on a mare nursing her foal.

Epona was worshipped at least from the first to the fifth centuries AD, and my view is that there may be a genuine connection between her and the Rhiannon of Welsh myth. In the Foretaste of this book, I explained how this might have happened, how early Christian travelling clerics might have seen still-standing images of Epona and then woven her into stories that entered the repertoire of early oral storytelling, these being ultimately written down in medieval texts. The connection between Epona and her horses is subtle and interesting: she is not herself depicted as a horse but she has a visceral association with her animal avatars.

SILVER AND SACRED WHEELS

Aranrhod's name is significant. Did 'silver wheel' refer to a celestial connection? Was she, perhaps, a moon-goddess in disguise, or a relic of an earlier pagan pantheon? In the western provinces of the Roman Empire, including Gaul and Britannia, there was a popular sky or solar cult associated with the god Taranis, or 'Thunderer'. Taranis's symbolism often included wheel images and symbols of the sun. One image of this male deity occurs on one of the narrative inner plates of the later Iron Age silver Gundestrup cauldron. A second of these plates depicts a scene in which a female sits between two wheels, as though she were riding in a chariot, a ceremonial cart, or even perhaps a bier. While, as remarked upon before, it would be folly to make a firm or direct link between this image and Aranrhod, it is possible that a fragment of memory might have percolated down through the centuries and have found its way into the repertoire of peripatetic storytellers. And while the character of Aranrhod belonged to Wales and the Gundestrup cauldron to Scandinavia, as mentioned in the previous chapter, there is the possibility that the cauldron began life as a commission by Gallic religious practitioners. If this is true then it would be plausible to argue for some form of connection between Aranrhod and the archaeology of ancient wheel-symbolism found on the cauldron.

It is tempting to make reference here to the legendary ancient British ruler, Boudica, Queen of the Iceni tribe in East Anglia. She is chronicled by Tacitus and the later writer Cassius Dio as having nearly robbed the Roman empire of the entire fledgling province of Britannia in her defeats of subsequent Roman military forces sent to fight

> her in AD 60/61. These classical writers described her as
> leading her army while riding in a chariot. If such a vehicle
> was actually used by her, it would probably have closely
> resembled the Iron Age chariots found by archaeologists in
> burial sites not only in eastern England but also Scotland
> and recently in west Wales. These chariots, including their
> wheels, were highly decorated with gleaming metalwork
> that would have caught the light, particularly when in
> motion, in a defiant display of muscular bravado.

wife' very clearly: Rhiannon and Branwen. Rhiannon had two 'faults'. The first was that she was deemed responsible for failing to conceive until three years had passed since her marriage to Pwyll. The second was that, once she had given birth to their baby boy, she was falsely accused of murdering and eating him by the women appointed to watch over the child at night, covering up their guilty slumber. Rhiannon is made into a prize scapegoat. Pwyll fell short of ordering her execution for infanticide but instead gave her the bizarre punishment of acting as a beast of burden. Only when the child was safely restored to them did the harmony of their marriage resume and last until the king's death.

The 'heroine' of the Second Branch, Branwen, was likewise a calumniated wife. This is not the only parallel made by the storyteller between her and Rhiannon. For Branwen, too, was castigated for her apparently barren state, until she finally conceived and gave birth to the hapless Gwern, destined to die in the fire at the hand of his uncle Efnisien. Her punishment was not for alleged infanticide but for being Welsh in an Irish royal household. The insult made to Matholwch, before his wedding, by Efnisien's mutilation of his horses still rankled in the hearts of Matholwch's courtiers, even after Brân's reconciliatory gift of his priceless cauldron had been gracefully accepted. Matholwch's men continued to grumble about the insult delivered by their new queen's brother, constantly reminding him of the slur to his royal status and the need to avenge the wrong. Branwen was an easy and convenient scapegoat to shoulder the blame for her brother's transgressions.

Branwen's punishment was as bizarre as Rhiannon's, although entirely different. She was banished from the court and her husband's bed and sent to work as the lowliest servant in the kitchen, where she was forced to cook for the court. What is more, the court butcher came to her every day, his hands bloodied from the meat he had been chopping, and gave her a clout round the ear.

Fearing that Brân would hear of Branwen's plight, Matholwch banned all travel by sea to Wales and announced that anyone travelling to Ireland would immediately be impounded and flung into prison. Thus Branwen was entirely cut off from outside aid. This continued for three years (yes, the magic three years again) until Branwen managed to send word to her brother via her trained starling. Despite her rescue, her ill-luck continued. She lost her only son, who burnt to death before her eyes. Then her despair at having caused such terrible harm to the Irish and Welsh nations pained her with such grief that her heart failed and she perished on the banks of the river Alaw.

There could be another influence other than misogyny that brought calumny upon prominent female protagonists, and that is xenophobia: the suspicion and hostility towards a foreigner. Branwen was Welsh and her husband was Irish. If there were genuine ancient tensions between Wales and Ireland, they might have coloured the way in which some things were presented in the tales. Why were Matholwch's people so against his new wife and consort? Might there have been a residue of resentment at work here? And something similar perhaps caused a storyteller to point the finger at Rhiannon. She might well have been perceived by Pwyll's people as dangerous. While she was not a foreigner as such, her strange first appearance in front of Pwyll made it clear that she that was not of this world. If she came from the realm of the spirits, she might well have been seen as odd by Pwyll's people, and it would have been easy to judge her guilty of the sin of infanticide if she were viewed as someone alien and therefore intrinsically suspect.

Dangerous women: betrayal and sexual perfidy

While Rhiannon and Branwen are portrayed as innocent victims, two prominent female characters who play major roles in the Fourth Branch are treated very differently. They are Aranrhod, the mother of Lleu Llaw Gyffes, and Blodeuwedd, his wife. And in the story of these two protagonists, Christian moral judgement is very clearly defined. Aranrhod presents herself to Math, lord of Gwynedd, as a virgin when her birth to two boys betrayed her. Blodeuwedd was not only unfaithful to her husband but also connived with her lover to murder him. But a third woman must also be remembered. She is Goewin, with her job as foot-holder to the king on account of her virginity. She also fell from grace but as a result of rape by Math's nephew Gilfaethwy.

First we will look at the story of Aranrhod. The character of Aranrhod is complex and contrary but sketchily developed in Welsh myth. She is presented as a candidate for the fallen Goewin's role as the royal foot-holder of Math. The king had called for would-be candidates but was determined not to be fobbed off by women falsely claiming to be virgins. And so he used a wand to establish whether the women were true maidens. Aranrhod failed dismally by giving birth to two baby boys as she stepped across the staff. She was not a virgin. While the firstborn, Dylan, disappeared, later to be murdered by Gofannon, the second was taken under the wing of Math's son, Gwydion. The child grew big and sturdy, developing much earlier than a normal human infant (surely displaying his superhumanity). But Aranrhod, angry and ashamed at this living testimony to her false claim, put the three spells on him, endeavouring to stop him acquiring manly status. She denied him a name, arms and marriage, all of which his kinsman Gwydion circumvented by magical trickery.

It may be that Gwydion saved Lleu partly on account of guilt, because he connived with his brother to allow Gilfaethwy's rape of the innocent Goewin. The story of Aranrhod glosses over the circumstances surrounding the father of her twin boys. But there is one theory that perhaps explains this mystery: the possible presence of an earlier lost version of the myth, where Aranrhod, like Goewin, had been raped, perhaps even by Gwydion. This would serve to explain

GENDER SUBVERSION IN
ROMANO-BRITISH ICONOGRAPHY

In her book *Women in Roman Britain*, Lindsay Allason-Jones wrote that, according to evidence from inscriptions, some Romano-British women possessed an identity that was germane specifically to them rather than to a husband or a father. This suggests that they had a measure of independence that differed from the strictures normally imposed upon Roman women (one exception being the Vestal Virgins, as described later in this chapter). Archaeological evidence from the Iron Age onwards displays the presence of powerful, high-status females and this is particularly evident in burial practices. Classical writers, such as Tacitus, speak of ruler-women in Britain at the time of the Roman occupation: Boudica and Cartimandua. The same does not appear to have been the case in Gaul – at least not as far as literary testimony is concerned – although Breton Iron Age coinage does include images of armed females riding horses or driving chariots. Iconography appears to confirm the prominence of females in traditional male roles, particularly that of a warrior. In Roman Britain, one particular image from the Cotswolds, the tribal territory of the Dobunni, expresses this gender-subversion. It was found at Lemington but probably came originally from the great Roman villa complex at Chedworth, which was not far from what would have been the Dobunnic capital at Cirencester. It depicts a schematically carved figure of a woman, her right hand resting on what appears to be a bucket, and in her left hand a spear. The image thus challenges norms in two ways as it presents both female warriorhood and sinistrality (left-handedness). Interestingly, the motif of left-handedness is repeatedly found on gold coins, where horsewomen are depicted galloping into battle, a shield in their right hand and a sword in their left. I have argued in an earlier publication, *An Archaeology of Images*, that the notion of the female soldier, and a left-handed one at that, is a deliberate subversion of *romanitas* (Romanness). A left-handed legionary infantryman in the Roman army would have been a disaster, for Roman soldiers' efficiency in battle depended upon operation as a single unit, using their shields in the left hand to defend each other's flank, and leaving the right arm free to wield the *gladius* (short sword). So the Lemington carving is doubly subversive and its sculptor (or the person who commissioned it) may have been making a point of Dobunnic Britishness.

why she repudiated her children and why Gwydion took such care of her second child, Lleu, in guarding him, revoking her curses upon him, and finally rescuing him from his murderous wife and her lover.

In order to place Blodeuwedd, Lleu's treacherous wife, in context, we need to look to his mother, Aranrhod. It was she who put a ritual embargo on her son's ability to acquire a wife (and therefore to procreate). She was clearly anxious that the line should terminate with him. Her resentment of him makes sense if her virginity had been taken from her by force. It was her curse that led to his tragic downfall because the only wife available to him was an ephemeral creation made out of flowers by the magic of Math and Gwydion.

It is pertinent to look a little more closely at this flower symbolism. The wild flowers chosen by Math and Gwydion in order to fashion a wife for Lleu were of three different kinds: oak, meadowsweet and broom. Oaks produce both male and female flowers that grow together on the same tree. The male flowers grow as long, dangling catkins and flower in April and May when their pollen is released. The female flowers are small, round and red and, once they are fertilised by the male pollen, they develop into acorns during the autumn. Unlike oaks, which flourish in forests, meadowsweet usually grows in wetland areas, such as water meadows and ditches, and it produces frothy white flowers between June and September. The bright yellow flowers of the broom shrub bloom between April and June. Broom likes coastal areas, hedgerows and open woodland habitats. So what kind of significance might be read into the choice made by Math and Gwydion for their conjuring of a woman of flowers to be Lleu's wife? Some scholars argue that meaning might be found in the fact that these plants flower at different times of the year, but that doesn't really work because there is overlap, particularly between meadowsweet and broom. It could be to do with the very obvious appearance of all three flower-bearing plants: oaks stand out in the landscape because of their size (and, of course, there is a link between oak flowers and the great oak into which Lleu, transformed into an eagle, flew); meadowsweet has distinctive clusters of white blooms; and broom flares bright yellow in the landscape. But I wonder whether the choice was perhaps connected to their differing habitats: forests, damp places, coastal places and hedgerows. If this were relevant, Blodeuwedd's origins might have signified symbolism that embraced the totality of the landscape, giving her existence particular potency. One other feature is shared by all three plants: their deciduous nature, suggestive of changefulness. Blodeuwedd was a temporary creature, unstable and fickle, which reflects that idea.

Maidenhood unwrapped

In so many cultures, past and present, virginity was and is an important issue. In ancient European societies, such as that of the Roman world, its significance is particularly marked in religion, as exemplified by the Vestal Virgins – women who renounced sex, marriage and children. They dressed in pure white, to signify their virgin status, and their role was to dwell in the temple of the goddess Vesta and tend her sacred fire, which was never allowed to go out. To be a Vestal had pluses and minuses. A plus was that she possessed many 'masculine' privileges denied other women, such as the ability to conduct business affairs without a male guardian. And, after thirty years' service as a Vestal, she was released from her 'bonds of virginity'. A minus was that, should she be found to have indulged in sexual activity during her years as a priestess of Vesta, she would be condemned to a horrible punishment: burial alive, with a little water and lamp-oil. She would be left to die a lingering, agonising death from thirst and starvation in the lonely darkness.

Celibacy was and is still a trenchant subject, not least in divine matters, as witnessed by its crucial role in Roman Catholicism for monks and nuns, who are deemed to belong to God and the Church rather than a human partner. I think that in a pagan setting, such as ancient Rome or in Welsh myth (in its pre-Christian origins), the significance of female virginity may have another dimension: that of being a source of undissipated sexual energy. The role of Math's foot-holder may be associated with the need for the king to have undisputed and unshared powers that were generated by Goewin's virgin state.

Subversive voices: problems with women

Welsh (and Irish) mythmakers exhibit a certain amount of contradictive and uncomfortable thinking when it comes to women. There is tension and misogyny in their characterisation, and powerful females were often given a fairly bad press because they flouted the norm. Peredur's witch who taught him warcraft is an excellent example of gender encroachment and the blurring of sexual boundaries.

When Rhiannon first appeared to Pwyll, she was riding on horseback and able to outride both him and his swiftest horsemen, which shows her to be different from the feminine norm. The storyteller explains this by according her divine status. And there is a further element to Rhiannon's power: she is able to choose her husband, rather than waiting to be selected by a suitor. She made it clear to Pwyll when they first met that she was making the first move towards their marriage, and this would have been somewhat alien to the usual custom of a man seeking out a wife.

Branwen seems utterly female, yet it was she who, albeit unwittingly, caused the great war between Wales and Ireland, with the consequence of catastrophic loss of life. Both Rhiannon and Branwen were castigated for their apparent barrenness. The 'villainesses', Aranrhod and Blodeuwedd, both flouted the given values of womanhood: chastity, honesty, fertility and fidelity – all strict Christian ethical principles.

IMAGING FEMALE BOUNTY

The descriptions of Rhiannon's and Branwen's largesse have certain parallels with religious iconography from Roman Britain. In a sense, these two mythic women expressed their fertility not only in both bearing a child but in their lavish distribution of presents to their guests. So it is interesting that a 'mother-goddess' cult – that clearly originated not in the Roman pantheon but in the western provinces of Britain, Gaul and the Rhineland – thrived in the north and west of England and also in south Wales. The cluster of such images found on artefacts in the Cotswolds, particularly in Cirencester and its environs, strongly indicates a centre for this cult here, among the Dobunni. The goddesses are usually depicted seated and frequently in triplicate. The triplism of these images resonates – though it is not necessarily directly linked – with the storyteller's description of Branwen as one of the 'Three Chief Maidens' in the land. The goddesses may nurse babies or interact with small children but, just as often, their carvings show them holding baskets of fruit or bread, as symbols of the earth's bounty. One example, from Daglingworth, near

Cirencester, bears a scratched name, 'Cuda', a British word alluding to prosperity or high regard. Another image was found in Wales, at Caerwent. This was the tribal capital of the Silures, the local tribe which fought so bitterly, and in vain, to retain its independence in the face of the advancing Roman army in the mid-to-later first century AD. This image of a Silurian goddess, dating to the second or third century AD, depicts her, not with children or food, but with a yew frond and an aril (a red yew berry), as if to represent longevity or the changing seasons. What I find particularly interesting is that the sculptor chose to use local sandstone for this carving, suggesting intention to represent the goddess's local identity, rather than using the grander Bath stone preferred by the Roman army for its inscriptions and depictions of Roman deities.

Wine, women and song

Having dwelt at length on the negative treatment of the heroine in Welsh myth, I want to end this chapter by looking at a positive take on two prominent female protagonists: Rhiannon and Branwen. Both women are presented as being bountiful and associated with plenty and gift-giving. Time and again in the First Branch, Rhiannon was closely associated with feasting. She was renowned for her generosity to her guests and, when she and Pwyll had their wedding feast, she was noted for not allowing any man or woman to leave the festivities without being presented with a precious present of jewellery. Branwen's story, in the Second Branch, contains an almost identical reference to her benefaction. Her initial encounters with the Irish king were closely associated with feasting. And when she arrived in Ireland as

Matholwch's bride, she gave every man or woman of high status a valuable piece of jewellery. The storyteller hints further at her bountiful nature by introducing her as 'One of the Three Chief Maidens of this Island'. After three years of barrenness, both women bore sons and both subsequently lost them. Rhiannon's story becomes woeful because of the loss of her child and her consequent unjust punishment, but all becomes right in the end. But Branwen's tale remains dark, ending with her young son being flung into the fire by Efnisien where he burns to death, and she eventually dies by suicide.

While, of course, not seeking to argue for direct association between the mother-goddess cult in Roman Britain and the 'heroic' women of Welsh myth, once again it seems highly likely that there could be a relic of folk memory that allowed stories to be influenced by traditions that circulated in western Britain much earlier – for example, to explain Rhiannon's horse-persona and the symbolism of regenerative cauldrons. In the two chapters that follow, we will explore other such threads: the significance of number and colour; and sacral kingship (or the divine marriage).

CHAPTER 7

Magic Numbers
and Mythic Colours

*'I was thinking about the woman I loved best. This is why I was
reminded of her: I was looking at the snow and at the raven and at
the drops of blood from the duck which the hawk had killed in the
snow. And I was thinking that the whiteness of her skin was like the
snow, and the blackness of her hair and eyebrows was like the raven,
and that the two spots in her cheeks were like the two drops of blood.'*

Taken from the tale 'Peredur, son of Efrog', this quotation is from the
eponymous hero's description of his lady and neatly brings together the
two themes of this chapter: triplism (or threeness) and colour. Both are
persistent threads running through most of the Welsh mythic stories.

The importance of colour is, I think, partly due to the oral origins
of the tales: word-painting is so greatly enhanced by giving it a colour-
wash. Gleaming white, dazzling gold, glowing red and sinister black
provide a vibrant backdrop to the stories themselves, instilling life
(and death) into them.

The theme of number is more perplexing, challenging and capable
of multifarious interpretations, dependent upon societal context. The
dominant number, used again and again by the myth-spinners, is three

Peredur battles with the
Nine Wicked Witches of Caer Loyw.

(and its multiple, nine). Other odd numbers, such as seven and five, also recur several times. Perhaps lurking behind different contextual thinking is the overarching theme of oddness. Numbers incapable of equal halving of themselves impose issues of instability, asymmetry, restlessness and oscillation. Take, as an example, the La Tène symbol known as the triskele, a three-armed whirligig, particularly common in Welsh late Iron Age decorated metalwork. One piece displaying this restless mobile image adorns a rectilinear bronze plaque from Moel Hiraddug in north Wales. Contained within a circle on the plaque (perhaps originally used to decorate a shield), the triskele spins vertiginously round into an ever-whirling vortex: the more you stare at it, the more it moves. It is tempting to see an object such as this as possessing secret, magical powers designed to protect its bearers and repel their enemies.

But triplism has a wide range of possibilities for interpretation. The Welsh mythic storytellers told of the 'three singing birds of Rhiannon', who was closely associated with the inexplicable phenomenon of otherworldliness. The manifestation of these birds in the tales (notably in the Second Branch and in 'Culhwch and Olwen') signified to their audience that those to whom they appeared were in connection with the spirit realm. Branwen, a central and catalystic figure in the Second Branch, is introduced as one of the 'Three Chief Maidens' or 'Three Chief Matriarchs' of the island of Britain (depending on the translation). Clearly it is contradictory to speak of her as maiden *and* matriarch but that need not concern us here: it is the threeness that is of interest. Later on, in the Fourth Branch, triplism recurs, for instance, in the three punishments visited upon Gwydion and Gilfaethwy by their uncle for besmirching his virgin foot-holder, Goewin. And there are far more references to the number three throughout the eleven tales that make up the *Mabinogion*.

Maidens and witches: three times three

Nine (perhaps a particularly potent number as it represents three times three) is also important in the myths, most prominently in descriptions of witches and virgins. In the early medieval poem *Preiddeu Annwfn* (*The Spoils of Annwfn*), the magical cauldron belonging to the strange otherworld is described as a truly magnificent vessel, studded with precious gems. No wonder that Arthur and his raiding band sought to acquire it and take it back to the land of the living. As we have seen earlier, like other Welsh mythic cauldrons, this was no ordinary kitchen utensil or mundane object used in cooking. It had attitude and made the choice to boil food for whom it wanted, and for no one else. As well as declining to stew meat for anyone accused of cowardice, it had very specific requirements for the fire used to heat it: it required the breath of nine virgins to fan the flames to the correct temperature. Why virgins? Perhaps, like Goewin who got her power from her undissipated and unused sexuality, these virgins were also perceived to hold that pure, undiluted potency in their expelled breath. And why nine of them? It is my contention that three times three not only multiplied threeness but concentrated it by tripling this symbolic number. According to this interpretation, it would still be triplism that held the magic but it was powerfully enhanced.

This may also account for the 'nineness' of the horrible witches of Gloucester encountered by the eponymous hero in 'Peredur, son of Efrog'. Peredur's story is shot through with the magical and sinister power of threeness. Following his arrival at the remote castle on a mountain, he was told by the countess about the dreadful Nine Witches of Caer Loyw who kept terrorising her and laying waste to all her lands. The triplication to nine witches served to intensify their capacity for menace and destruction. And the pitting of a single hero against nine malign forces would have thrilled the storyteller's audiences. How could one person alone triumph over nine supernatural women? Of course, after a drilling in warcraft – ironically by one of the witches herself – Peredur emerged as a hero whose essential goodness overcame evil. And in that, we are reminded, perhaps, of David and Goliath.

Singing birds and stolen babies

Rhiannon, wife of Pwyll (in the First Branch) and of Manawydan (in the Third), has a close link with horses. But she also has a connection with birds and possesses three magical singing birds. The birds had the power both to wake the dead and to lull the living to sleep, once more emphasising their otherworld status and, indeed, Rhiannon's.

Towards the end of the Second Branch of the *Mabinogi*, Brân's grieving companions and his sister, Branwen, travelled to Harlech, taking with them the severed (but still sentient and talking) head of their chieftain. They arrived at Harlech where a feast awaited them. As they began to take food and drink, three birds were heard in the dining hall singing Brân's company a song – the sweetest any of them had ever heard. These were the singing birds of Rhiannon, and they were magical because, although their song was crystal clear to the listeners in the hall, the birds themselves were so far out at sea that even those with the keenest sight struggled to see them. The sojourn of Brân's men in Harlech, during which they continued to feast, lasted for seven years before they made the journey to Gwales (the island of Grassholm) in Pembrokeshire. There they remained, with Brân's head, for a further eighty years, before taking it to its final resting place in London. The triadic symbolism of this tale presents itself in other ways, too, including the description of Branwen's punishment at King Matholwch's hand, which sparked the great war between Ireland and Wales, as 'One of the Three Unfortunate Blows'. Interestingly, the story of Brân is not the only place where Rhiannon's birds are mentioned. In 'Culhwch and Olwen', one of the 'impossible tasks' demanded of Culhwch and Arthur's company by Olwen's father, Ysbaddaden, was to find for him the singing birds of Rhiannon.

There is a significant link between the singing birds of Welsh myth and depictions of the otherworld in the medieval Irish legends. The Irish otherworld was a place often perceived as located across the sea. It was where life after death was depicted as the land of the living, and where sickness was unknown. In some tales, this magical place was filled with wonderful music sung by birds with dazzling plumage. Furthermore, it was a land where the very trees sang, instruments played on their own and the very stones reverberated with enchanted music. The Irish otherworld was also peopled with numerous beautiful women. And so, Welsh oral storytellers might have been influenced by others from across the Irish Sea, their own stories of Rhiannon and her singing birds sharing the common themes of fabulous women, birds and music with Ireland.

Another repeated triadic theme in Welsh oral tales is kidnapped infants, with the additional inference being that malign spirit-forces were at work. In 'Culhwch and Olwen', another of the 'impossible tasks' laid upon Culhwch was to locate Mabon (meaning 'the young son'). He had been stolen from his mother Modron (meaning literally 'mother') when he was 'three nights old' (this way of counting time was common in Gaul and noted by Julius Caesar in *De Bello Gallico*), but had grown up and earned the reputation for being the greatest hunter in the world. As we saw earlier in this book, Mabon was found imprisoned in Gloucester Castle, and released by Culhwch and Arthur to accompany them on their quest to secure Olwen's hand in marriage. Rhiannon and Pwyll's baby son is also stolen. He vanished during the night of his birth but materialised in the stable belonging to Teyrnon and his wife. This couple brought him up as their own. As he grew, the child's resemblance to Pwyll became so marked that the pair, knowing about the baby's kidnap, decided this must be the missing boy and that he must be restored to his birth parents. Teyrnon's wife states that their reward for giving up the child would be threefold: gratitude from Rhiannon for freeing her from her penance; thanks from Pwyll both for raising and cherishing the boy as their own; and the hope and expectation that the lad himself, when grown to manhood, would remain their foster-son and would look favourably upon them when he took over the lordship of Dyfed. Here, triplism was connected with the return of a stolen child.

Triple penance: Gwydion and Gilfaethwy

It is quite likely that storytellers used particular tropes or triggers upon which to hang their tales as a marker to alert and prepare listeners (and later readers) to a significant happening about to unfold. Maybe the number three was one of these. The compendium of Welsh stories known as the *Trioedd Ynys Prydein* (the *Triads of the Island of Britain*) was compiled in written form in the twelfth century and would certainly have been known to those who wrote down the myths. This collection might very well have been influenced by earlier oral storytellers.

In the Second Branch, Branwen is introduced as one of three maidens or matriarchs and, interestingly, her story ends with a plethora of triads. The burial of her brother Brân's head in London was referred to as one of the 'Three Fortunate Concealments' and then as one of the 'Three Unfortunate Disclosures' when the head's presence was revealed to Brân's men. And Branwen's punishment by her husband and her untimely death from a broken heart is mentioned as one of the 'Three Unfortunate Blows'.

The references to 'unfortunate disclosures' and 'unfortunate blows' bring me to look at other examples of a negative triadic device. In the Fourth Branch, a triple punishment was meted out to Gwydion and Gilfaethwy by Math for their perfidy in causing a war and defiling his foot-holder, Goewin, thus depriving Math of a source of his power. The king used his magic to turn the young men into three different pairs of animals – wolves, deer and wild pigs – a male and female of each. The vengeful magician's curse meant that the brothers had to mate with each other, in their animal forms, as a further punishment for Goewin's stolen virginity. Another such triadic curse was visited upon Aranrhod's infant son, also in the Fourth Branch, in her attempt to deny him a name, arms upon coming of age, and a wife.

Triplism has another significant manifestation – very widespread in traditional (and particularly shamanistic) communities past and present – in the notion of the three-layered cosmos, which we explored in Chapter 3. These cosmic layers were not deemed to be specifically physical entities with physical boundaries but were metaphorical realms of being whose borders could be broached by shamans, who had a 'key' to the other worlds. It might be a fanciful notion but not impossible that the triplism so persistent in some of the myths (and, of course, in the earlier iconography of Britain) could contain a germ of this kind of belief structure. The triple nature of so many punishments described in the myths may, of course, have nothing to do with shamanic cosmologies. However, it is possible that a lurking folk memory of the power of three imbued this number with such symbolic potency that it percolated through to the tales, giving the punitive actions particular muscle.

ARCHAEOLOGIES OF THREENESS

Triplism appears to have been an endemic part of British and European Iron Age and Roman provincial symbolism. Variations on the theme of three appear over and over again on Iron Age coinage. A prime example is the triple-tailed horse that was chosen as a favourite image on gold coins minted by the Dobunni of the Cotswold region. The tribe of the Silures in south Wales does not seem to have minted its own coinage but several of these triple-tailed-horse coins found their way (either as trade items or as part of an exchange of gifts) into Silurian territory. I have already mentioned the three-armed whirligig (triskele) found on the bronze plaque from Moel Hiraddug, which is only one example of several found on Iron Age Welsh military metalwork. Perhaps one of the most evocative other examples decorates the bronze crescent-shaped plaque from the votive hoard at Llyn Cerrig Bach on Anglesey. The 'arms' of this object's triskele terminate in what appear to be birds' heads. This piece may once have adorned a shield or even a chariot and so may even have witnessed battles between local north Welsh communities and the Roman army. And the fact that this object was found in water (in a mire) is significant, for the site of Llyn Cerrig Bach might have been a druidic sanctuary and possibly one specifically mentioned in the writings of Tacitus. It may be considered far-fetched, but I am tempted to imagine that the depiction of the triple bird on the Llyn Cerrig Bach plaque could perhaps be a forerunner of Rhiannon's birds, and have influenced an orally circulating myth long before the medieval legends were written down.

The cult of the mother-goddesses was also widespread, and is often combined with triplism and expressed in the iconography of three women. They are generally seated side by side, with babies, bread or fruit. These deities were not Roman in origin but originated among local populations in Britannia, Gallia (Gaul) and the Rhineland. The cult appears to have been popular in western Britain, particularly in the Cotswolds, with centres of worship clustered in and around Corinium (Cirencester), the tribal capital of the Dobunni. In some iconography, the figures appear to represent the three ages of womanhood: youth, maturity and old age. It is tempting to make connections between these triplistic female stone images and the description of Branwen, as one of the 'Three Chief Matriarchs (or Maidens)' of Britain. Notwithstanding the chronological discrepancies between the Roman-period iconography and a medieval mythic character, it is still possible that a long-lived oral tradition of storytelling might have played a role in uniting traditions over long periods. It is equally possible that some of these stone images were still visible in the post-Roman landscape when the later tales were circulating.

Colouring it in: red, white and black

The opening quote for this chapter sees Peredur speak of his lady, singling out the colours of red, white and black to describe her beauty. In previous chapters, we have drawn numerous connections between the mythologies of Wales and Ireland, and they also share a symbolism in colour. This scene, where Peredur admired his true love's colouring – black hair, white skin and red cheeks – is a remarkably similar (but reversed) image from the early Ulster myth the *Táin Bó Cuailnge*, in the story of the lovers Deirdre and Naoise. Often referred to as 'Deirdre of the Sorrows', Deirdre was destined to bring woe upon

Ulster, even while she was still an unborn infant. The druid Cathbad prophesied that her stunning beauty would wreak disaster. So terrified of the prophecy were they, that the men of Ulster begged the king, Conchobar, to have the baby killed at birth. But the king could not bring himself to murder the child and, instead, brought Deirdre up in secret as his foster-daughter, hiding her away so that she could do no harm. But as she reached puberty, her beauty blossomed and Conchobar himself desired to marry her. But one winter's day, the girl caught sight of her foster-father killing and skinning a calf, its bright blood staining the snow and a coal-black raven drinking the spilt gore. At the sight of the three colours, the maiden made a vow that the man she chose to wed would have raven hair, white skin and red cheeks. She found her would-be husband, Naoise, and – despite his initial reluctance – she persuaded him to elope with her. This brought down the wrath of Conchobar. He broke a pledge to spare the boy, murdering him at his court, leading to a bitter and bloody conflict between the king's men and the company of Ferghus, the envoy who had innocently lured Naoise to his death.

The parallels between these Irish and Welsh stories did not end there. Peredur's love for his raven-haired maiden also led to a lot of killing. Like Deirdre, this girl was also sequestered and jealously guarded by her father and his company of giants. To me, the tales, each with their red, white and black love themes, are too similar to be happenstance, and hint loudly at a shared vein of storytelling. Could it be that the 'clash of colours' contained a deep-rooted symbolism evocative of the horrors of war? After all, battlefields are full of spilt red blood and gore, white bones and blackened, decayed flesh.

Just for a few lines, I want to digress into something anthropological. In parts of central Africa, notably among the Ndembu people of the Democratic Republic of the Congo, the triadic linkage between red, white and black is of considerable significance. For Ndembu communities, this colour triad holds very specific emotional, social, religious, aesthetic and moral values. For anyone living outside Central Africa, the fluidity of interpreting these values is difficult to grasp. The closest we can come to a conclusion is to say that white and red could stand for life, and red also for death, while black seems to have been connected firmly to death.

White and black are antithetical but it is red that is especially interesting because it is often paired with white. It is as if this triadic structure is restless, unstable and needs to be resolved with pairing. Earlier in this chapter, I made reference to just this kind of instability in the asymmetry of triads in the Welsh mythic tales (which may also be reflected in earlier British cult imagery, such as that of the mother-goddesses).

These triadic, juxtaposed colours are interesting. All three can symbolise aspects of the body's death and decomposition: the red of blood, the black of putrefaction, and the end-product: white bones. In her book *Controlling Colours: Function and Meaning of Colour in the British Iron Age*, Dr Marlies Hoecherl explores, in depth, the connections between red, black and white in later prehistoric societies. Decay itself has several colour stages: firstly black putrefaction (with its odour of rotting meat). This stage is followed by the process called butyric fermentation, when the body gradually dries out after the decaying flesh, including skin and ligaments, have been devoured by flies and beetles. The remains become covered with a whitish mould that gives off its own cheesy smell. Only after that process do the bleached bones emerge, and the remains eventually become odourless. In some societies, where the bodies of deceased relatives remain exposed, sometimes within houses or on excarnation platforms, the colours of death might be perceived as closely associated with the varied smells involved in their dissolution. And it is striking that several early prehistoric burials involved the bodies being ritually covered in red ochre. For example, the Upper Palaeolithic 'Red Lady of Paviland', which was actually the body of a young man (his slightly built skeleton mistakenly suggesting to the body's early-nineteenth-century discoverers that he was a young woman), was laid to rest in a remote cave on Gower some 25,000 years ago. Perhaps this kind of act not only reflected the colour of blood but also the prospect of reincarnation in the otherworld.

So far, this discussion has featured only inhumation burials. But colours are also important in the disposal of bodies by cremation. Once again, the colour triad of red, white and black is present: in the red of fire; the black of charcoal, charred wood and human remains; and the whitish-grey of calcined bones or ash. The smells generated here would also vary, according to the stage: the early decomposition of a body awaiting the funeral pyre, the odour of burning flesh and the odourless or less pungent smell of cremated remains.

Colours in the Welsh mythic otherworld

Colour references within Annwfn, the otherworld ruled by Arawn, introduced in the First Branch and cited in many other tales, are interesting. Black might be expected to be the primary shade of this realm but it isn't. Pwyll, prince of Dyfed, was first confronted by Arawn in a quarrel over a hunted deer, after the mortal lord's encounter with Arawn's hounds, which came to the upper world with their master. Professor Sioned Davies's superb translation of the *Mabinogion*, published in 2007, contains an index of place names including Annwfn, which she translates as 'the in-world'. This term signifies that this place is separate from the material world of humans and difficult to access. Arawn's hounds, the *cwn Annwfn*, are described as very distinctive in appearance: they were dazzling white but with bright red ears – colours which identified them as otherworldly creatures. An idea of mine, which could be dismissed as overly fanciful, is whether the red ears might be a reference to blood and death. This would be appropriate enough for hunting dogs whose ears, perhaps, were deemed as being dipped in blood. The colour combination of Arawn's hounds reflects yet another mythic link with Ireland, whose tales also speak of white and red as otherworldly colours – particularly red. The '*Togail Bruidne Da Derga*' ('Tale of Da Derga's Hostel') is steeped in redness. Da Derga means red-gold and, in this story, the otherworld is red, as were many of its creatures, particularly its horses. The 'hero' of the Irish tale was a king named Conaire, whose doom was sealed when he broke a *geis*, a kind of injunction or prohibition, against the killing of birds.

Although she is thought to have come to Dyfed from the Welsh otherworld, Rhiannon's horse was not red but a gleaming white steed. The otherworld animals in the *Mabinogion* were all dazzling white. Another good example is the huge shimmering white boar, in the Third Branch, which showed itself to the hunting dogs of Pryderi and Manawydan in a thicket, and made their hackles rise in terror. It was this white boar that lured the dogs and Pryderi to a magic fort, clearly a manifestation of the otherworld. As noted in Chapter 3, boars were often used to bridge the divide between the mundane world and 'underland'. Arawn, lord of Annwfn, gave Pryderi (and Wales) the gift of swine. A sow led Gwydion to Lleu, stricken by enchantments and at death's door. And, of course, a pivotal character in 'Culhwch and Olwen' was Twrch Trwyth, a king changed into a great enchanted boar by God. Interestingly, one of his shape-changed companions, a boar named Grugyn Gwrych Eraint, was described by the storyteller as having brilliant silver-white bristles that glittered so brightly that they would light up the deepest forest.

For the most part, the colour black is given a bad press by Welsh myth-spinners. An exception is the admiration for raven-haired young women. But usually, black seems to have been almost a synonym for ugliness and/or evil. Swarthy people were often perceived as not good, and witches, too, were often painted as dark and dangerous. The story of Ceridwen's cauldron exemplifies this connection with the colour black. Ceridwen's son was named Afagddu, which means 'black' or 'ugly'. Conversely, her other son is called Crearwy meaning 'light' or 'beautiful'. So, as is sadly still the case in many societies, people light of skin (and sometimes hair) were favoured over their opposites. After Afagddu is cheated of his birthright, the elixir of wisdom, it is no accident that Gwion, who inadvertently received this gift, was eventually reborn as Taliesin which means the 'bright, shining one'. He is in stark contrast to the one robbed of his mother Ceridwen's promised precious gift.

'Peredur, son of Efrog' is a tale full of colour, and the storyteller used black to signify to their audience that something (or someone) unpleasant was about to occur in the narrative. One of the several maidens the eponymous hero encountered warned him of a forest in a dangerous place called the Round Valley. She told Peredur that there were black houses in which dwelt her father's vassals – all of them murderous giants who planned to slaughter him. On another occasion, the hero was out hunting near Caerleon when he spotted a house in the distance and decided to stop there. In the hall he could see three bald-headed, swarthy young men playing the chess-like board game *gwyddbwyll*. One of three maidens who had been sitting watching the game began to cry. When Peredur asked what had upset her, she replied that she was weeping because he was about to be murdered by her father, the lord of the court. He had the habit of killing anyone who came to his hall uninvited. Suddenly, this man appeared: he was huge and swarthy, with jet-black hair and only one eye. The maiden persuaded her father not to be hasty, so Peredur was safe for one night. The next day, he challenged

THE RED WOMAN OF WETWANG

The beginning of this millennium saw the discovery of a new Iron Age chariot-burial at Wetwang in East Yorkshire. The body, buried with a two-wheeled vehicle, was that of a woman of about thirty-five to forty years old, who had given birth to at least one child. She was clearly of high rank, indicated not only because of her chariot but also her other grave goods. These included the remains of joints of pork (a high-status food) that had been placed on her torso and a mirror placed across her lower legs. In late Iron Age Britain, mirrors in tombs signified a particular value. Often found in the graves of women, it is possible that their presence indicated that their possessors had enjoyed a special, possibly ritualistic, status. The back of these objects, and sometimes also their handles, are frequently highly ornamented in La Tène artistic motifs.

A striking thing about the metal objects found in the Wetwang woman's grave was the profusion of red coral and enamel that decorated the horse trappings, including the harness-fittings and bridle-bits. The glue holding the various pieces of horse fittings together was a black tar made from birch and pine. But the most distinctive element in this burial was revealed in study of the woman's facial bones. She had suffered from a tumour, tentatively identified as a facial haemangioma, a large, lumpy growth of wayward blood vessels that would have disfigured her face and been bright red in colour. Surely, it is not preposterous to suggest that this affliction was in some way acknowledged, even celebrated, by the inclusion of the red coral and enamel adornment in her grave. Far from being shunned by her community, this woman enjoyed the highest of ranks not only in life but also in death and the afterlife. In the words of Professor Melanie Giles, she was perhaps perceived as having been 'enamelled by the gods'. The colour triad of red, white and black was represented in her living body, her grave goods and, eventually, her skeleton.

the giant to single combat and bested him. The young hero told the giant that he would spare him if he explained how he had come to lose his eye. The giant replied that his eye was lost fighting the Black Serpent of the Cairn, and that he had been named the Black Oppressor because of his murderous nature.

There are more times, in the story of Peredur, where darkness and ugliness were combined with the colour black. There is a scene at Arthur's court at Caerleon, where four of his company sat together in the hall conversing, when a maiden suddenly approached. She was black, with curly hair and was riding on a yellow mule. Her facial expression was sour. The storyteller used all his word-painting powers to describe her villainous appearance. Her hands and face were blacker than pitch-smeared iron, and her misshapen ugliness, which surpassed her blackness, meant that she had sagging cheeks, flared nostrils, with one bulging green eye and the other black and sunken. She was crooked and bent over, with yellow teeth and a belly that reached higher than her chin. Despite her formidable appearance and surly, aggressive manner, she had a message for Arthur and his men, and told them that a maiden, immured in a castle, needed to be rescued. This messenger was clearly meant to be someone horrific and terrifying but, at the same time, she was on a mission of mercy, albeit one that would require warfare and bloodletting to resolve. Her description reminds me very much of scenes in the Irish 'Tale of Da Derga's Hostel'. The hostel is visited by the living human king Conaire, who saw there a nightmare figure: an old woman with a noose around her neck, wearing a striped cloak. Her long legs were black as coal, her mouth was at the side of her head, and she had a long, knee-length beard. She uttered prophecies to Conaire while standing on one leg. Both women – from Welsh and Irish myth respectively – were described in such an imaginative manner as to shock their audience – to give them goosebumps and cause their hair to stand on end.

Welsh myth-spinners used colour, literally, as a word-painting ploy, to mesmerise their audiences with stark images that they could picture in their mind's eye. As well as white, red and black, gold and auburn were used to represent riches and youth, and grey was used to reflect maturity or old age. Colours were vigorously employed in order both to entertain and to drive home moral statements concerning good and evil. Whatever the mindsets of the storytellers, whether by oral or written means, the result was the presentation of an incredibly rich tapestry of images. Listeners (or readers) would be aware of the meanings behind colour-coding and understand that they could anticipate a love-story, a forthcoming battle, a feast, a murder, witchery or an encounter with unsullied maidenhood. Colour was used here as a blazing beacon of imaginative storytelling and, of course, colour-coding remains highly relevant today. We still tend to dress baby girls in pink and boys in blue. Villains in popular culture – such as Darth Vader in the *Star Wars* films – often wear black, while heroes are more likely to be dressed in red, like Spider-Man or blue, like Superman. So colour continues to have as powerful a role in the modern world, whether in gender-symbolism or in storytelling, as it possessed in the world of mythic Wales.

Pwyll tries in vain to catch up with Rhiannon
on her shining white horse.

CHAPTER 8

Love, Marriage and Sacral Kingship

Pwyll sat upon the mound. And as they were sitting down, they
could see a lady on a big fine pale white horse, with a garment
of shining gold upon her, coming along the highway that led
past the mound ... 'Lady,' said he, 'wilt thou tell me anything of
thine errands?' 'I will, between me and God,' said she. 'My main
errand was to try and see thee ... I am Rhiannon daughter of
Hyfaidd the Old, and I am being given to a husband against my
will. But no husband have I wished for, and that out of love for
thee, nor will I have him even now unless thou reject me.'

Pwyll and Rhiannon's first meeting comes as he sits atop the sacred
Gorsedd Arberth, the magical mound that has the reputation of either
endowing any high-born man sitting upon it with a wonder or inflicting
a blow upon him. Rhiannon rides a strange horse that ambled sedately
along, while also outpacing all who pursued it. Rhiannon's encounter
with Pwyll is highly significant, for it was not only hedged about with
magic and otherworldliness, but it also put Rhiannon in charge of the
relationship between them. Rhiannon wielded the power that allowed
her to choose or reject a marriage partner. Although she was already

IMAGING WHITE HORSES
AND GREAT QUEENS

We have noted the importance of horses in late pre-Roman and Romano-British religious contexts – particularly with reference to the ancient horse-goddess Epona – in earlier chapters. And there is a piece of Roman iconography that specifically represents a white horse. This is an image depicted on a small shard of 'Castor ware' (polychrome painted pottery, so-named after the East Anglian potteries around Castor that produced it). The shard was found at Wroxeter, previously capital of the ancient British tribe of the Cornovii in Shropshire. It shows a bucking white horse on a black background. The horse is a fabulous, rearing beast, its eyes are staring, and its ears are flat as though it is galloping at full tilt. Its bridle and saddle-straps are picked out in grey dots, and its mane is similarly depicted in a double row of white circles which are stark against the black paint surrounding it. Was this just a decorative motif on a utilitarian pot or might it have carried some ritual significance?

That there was some kind of horse-cult at Wroxeter is reinforced by the discovery of an equine stone figure from a temple and a small clay-pipe figurine of a stallion. Remnants of a Jupiter column were also found here. These monuments, common in Roman Gaul, the Rhineland and with a few examples in Britain, are so-called because they are tall stone pillars, dedicated to the Roman sky-god. At their summit there was the image of a horseman, his mount's hooves trampling a human-faced underworld monster.

Although the themes of 'sacral kingship' and the goddess of sovereignty are much more muted and subtle in the Welsh tales than in Irish mythic tradition, they are present, albeit in a more nuanced form. Rhiannon's name is derived from another goddess, Rigantona, meaning 'great' or 'divine queen', who may have been worshipped in Roman times. A possible candidate for this early goddess can be found on the small, simply carved stone altar from Lemington in Gloucestershire (which probably belonged originally to the great Roman villa complex of Chedworth), that we encountered earlier in the book. The spear that she carried in her left hand was, perhaps, designed to represent potency rather than war. Both that and the vat or bucket (similar to those found on other stone images of local Cotswold goddesses) that her right hand rests upon could be seen as symbols of sovereignty. The spear represents dominance and the vessel might indicate her role as provider of bounty. Her identity as a deity is reinforced by the inscribed dedication on the base of the stone. It reads *'Dea Riigina'* – the 'Queen Goddess'. *'Riigina'* is a British-language version of 'Regina', and thus reflects her identity as a divinity belonging to the local tribe, the Dobunni. Could this goddess have been a forebear for Rhiannon – a mythic hero who enjoyed a reputation for generosity and plenty at her and Pwyll's court at Arberth?

betrothed to someone, she was able to flout the normal medieval male prerogative of choice (this choice was usually made by a woman's father and her suitor) and make her own selection of a husband.

A dominant theme in the early myths of Ireland is the idea of 'sacral kingship', wherein a mortal king married the 'goddess of sovereignty' who personified the land, thus legitimising his rule. It is highly likely, though less obvious, that Rhiannon's marriage to Pwyll meant something similar. Her – and her horse's – appearance to Pwyll, her gleaming gold garments and her mount's dazzling whiteness all strike a chord with Irish mythic tradition, suggesting that she and her horse emanated from the spirit world.

The goddess of sovereignty and the white mare

The treatise *Topographica Hibernica* (*The Topography of Ireland*) was written in 1185, by the cleric, Gerald of Wales (Giraldus Cambrensis). Gerald claimed that 'I completely wasted my time when I wrote my *Topography of Ireland* for Henry II, King of the English.' He made this comment because King Henry had virtually no interest in literature and, in any case, he was preoccupied with affairs of state. Gerald was of Norman-Welsh (three parts Norman, one part Welsh) extraction, having been born at Manorbier in Pembrokeshire. He held the high office of archdeacon of Brecon, and the post of royal clerk, which gave him the opportunity to travel widely. In the book, he described a royal inauguration ceremony that took place in Ulster, to symbolise the ritual union between the king and the goddess of sovereignty. It is unclear whether Gerald witnessed this Ulster ceremony or heard it from another source. But what is interesting, in the context of Rhiannon's appearance to Pwyll (and her link with horses), is that, in the ritual Gerald recorded, the goddess was represented not as a human woman but as a white mare. The king played the part of a stallion, symbolically mating with his equine partner. Afterwards, the white horse was killed, her flesh butchered and boiled in a cauldron until cooked, whereupon the king sat himself down inside the vessel, with the meat and broth and ate and drank of its contents until sated. So here, consumption of flesh appears to be equated with the sexual act. Odd indeed!

Sacral sovereignty and sacred bulls

In Chapter 3 of this volume, we looked at the Welsh tale known as 'Rhonabwy's Dream' where the eponymous hero lay down on a yellow ox-skin and was granted a series of visions while he slept. Although muted in tone, it is possible that Rhonabwy's sleep on his ox-hide refers obliquely to an old ritual that is chronicled in a number of Irish

A BULL-RITUAL AT GUNDESTRUP

The great silver cult-cauldron, made in the first century BC and found deposited in a peatbog in Jutland, has already appeared a number of times in this book. The striking image on the base plate of this vessel is a dying bull. The two holes on the top of his head were for detachable horns, perhaps made of real horn, and they may have been deliberately removed in ritual events to symbolise the animal's death. The image-rich cauldron would once have been used in religious ceremonies associated with feasting. And when the vessel was filled – with broth, boiled meat, blood or other substances – the twin horns might well have jutted out above the surface of the contents in a dramatic and repeated 'reincarnation' of the bull. Although the cauldron's final resting-place, as a votive deposition, was made in Denmark, its iconography suggests that it may have been looted by the local Cimbrian tribe on one of their raids in Gaul at roughly the same time as the cauldron is believed to have been made, in the second–first century BC.

The dying bull on the Gundestrup cauldron's base plate was not the only image of a bull to adorn it. One of the narrative, inner plates bears a scene of three identical bulls, each in the act of being sacrificed. It is likely that these represent the same bull but in triplication, perhaps to signify the sacred nature of the beast and of the number three. It might be far-fetched to hazard any kind of genuine link between the sacred stories told on the Gundestrup cauldron and the early historical mythic tales of Wales and Ireland, but a connection should not, in my opinion, be dismissed out of hand.

myths. This was called the *Tarbhfhess*, the 'bull-sleep' or 'bull-feast', that was a central part of kingship-election rituals in early Ireland and centred on the ceremonial and royal site of Tara in County Meath. During this sacro-political event, a candidate for elevation to the throne was chosen by means of a complicated ceremony wherein a bull was sacrificed and a selected male individual would then feast on the cooked meat and broth from the sacrificial victim. After this person had eaten and drunk his fill, he lay down to sleep while four druids chanted over him. As he slept, the rightful king to rule in Tara was revealed to him in a dream. When he woke up, he told the priests of his vision and, as they had the power to ascertain that he spoke the truth, so the new king would be elected.

While the connection between this ancient Irish ceremony and Rhonabwy's dream may be an indirect one, it is possible that – as already noted with other links between Welsh and Irish myth – this pagan *Tarbhfhess* might have been an influence in the later body of Welsh storytelling. And could it be that both the Welsh and Irish strands built upon earlier pagan traditions, as witnessed in the importance of bulls in Iron Age and Roman-period Britannia and Europe?

Marriage in myth: happiness and sorrow

In many of the Welsh mythic tales, the themes of falling in love, marriage, harmony and disharmony are explored. Some unions, like those of Pwyll and Rhiannon and then (after Pwyll's death) Rhiannon and Manawydan, are described as happy, even though both marriages were beset with vicissitudes, especially the first. Pwyll appears to have been a steadfast husband, despite their initial inability to produce offspring and even following the false rumours about his wife, when Rhiannon finally gave birth to their baby son only to have him go missing on the very night of his birth. It is interesting that Pwyll died and Rhiannon remarried and that there is no account of her demise. This, perhaps, reinforces her identity as an immortal goddess who (in Insular tradition at least) sometimes had a series of mortal royal husbands. Pwyll suffered pressure from his people, both to denounce her when she failed to conceive and to put her to death after the false accusation that she had slaughtered and eaten her son; he did neither, though she was punished for the latter.

Readers will recall that, before Pwyll met Rhiannon, he had a year's sojourn in the otherworld, after he swapped places with Annwfn's lord, Arawn. This is interesting in many ways but not least because of the relationship between Pwyll and Arawn's wife during his time in Annwfn. Pwyll had clearly taken on the otherworld lord's appearance and demeanour, for Arawn's queen had no idea that her husband had changed places with a mortal man. She and Pwyll conversed and feasted together, and they got on splendidly. But the queen was puzzled because, when they went to bed at night, he forbore to have intercourse with her. Instead he turned his back on her, edging as far away from her as possible, to avoid temptation. When the year was up, Pwyll returned to his princedom of Dyfed and Arawn returned to his otherworld realm. Arawn made love to his wife when they went to bed together and she was astonished, expressing her bewilderment at his change of attitude towards her. Only then did Arawn realise the honour Pwyll had done him by refraining from sex with his queen, and he praised him to the skies.

Both Rhiannon and Branwen were feted for their generosity to guests, both in terms of providing lavish food and drink at feasts and for dispensing precious gifts to those who visited their royal courts. However, Branwen's fate was very different from Rhiannon's. Although loved by her brother, Brân, the same could not be said of her husband, Matholwch, who was alienated by their brother Efnisien's insult to him in mutilating the Irish king's horses when he came to ask for her hand in marriage. In a sense, though, there is another similarity between the two women's stories: there appears to have been a whiff of xenophobia in both Pwyll's and Matholwch's courts towards their brides. Pwyll's men were quick to condemn his 'foreign' wife for being infertile, while the people of Matholwch's Irish court held Efnisien's insult over Branwen even though her husband had been mollified.

The saddest marriage in the myths is chronicled in the Fourth Branch of the *Mabinogion*: that between Lleu Llaw Gyffes and his flower-woman wife, Blodeuwedd. The misery was all the fault of his mother, Aranrhod, who spurned him from his birth and issued the

CUDA, GODDESS OF PLENTY

Rhiannon's and Branwen's reputation for their bounty and success reminds me of the Romano-British sculpture from the Dobunnic tribal capital of Corinium (Cirencester) that is dedicated to 'Cuda', the name etymologically linked to our word 'kudos', a term borrowed from the ancient Greek *ku-dos*, meaning 'praise' or 'renown' because of an achievement that benefits people. The inscribed dedication accompanies a sculpture depicting a seated mother-goddess, who holds an object in her lap which is either a loaf or an egg. She sits in a high-backed chair (itself reflective of high rank) and is receiving a gift from one of three little hooded figures, known as *Genii Cucullati* (see Chapter 7). The female figure is usually interpreted as a divinity but it is possible that she was a bountiful earthly queen receiving votive gifts and that the three hooded beings represent her subjects.

three prohibitions against him: denying him a name, arms and a wife. The curses laid upon the boy were then circumvented by his uncle, the magician Gwydion, aided by the latter's own uncle, Math, lord of Gwynedd. It was the overturning of the third curse that led to Lleu's downfall, with the conjuring of Blodeuwedd, the woman of flowers, to be Lleu's wife. She was a wayward, non-human being who was not only unfaithful to him but plotted to bring about his death. Lleu survived the attempt on his life by his wife's lover, and was eventually saved again by virtue of Gwydion's intervention but as a shadow of his former self. His wife was condemned to live her solitary life as an owl, hunting in the dark, as punishment. A great deal of symbolism is packed into this tale, threaded through as it is by Christian values: chastity, fidelity and truth. Blodeuwedd flouted all three because she was not a real person but woven from a magic spell, so she lacked the grounding upon which humanity was deemed to be built. The storyteller, probably a Christian, appears to have deliberately told a tale that warned listeners (and, later, readers) not to stray from the paths of righteousness. Marriage was sacred and the flouting of its rules threatened grave consequences, not least to the wronged partner, whom not even powerful pagan magic could restore to full humanity.

Passing the goblet: legitimising sacred kingship

In Irish mythology, the marriage between the goddess of sovereignty and the mortal king was sealed by her passing him a goblet of liquor. A prime example of this ceremony is the union between Ériu, the goddess personifying the land of Ireland, and the mortal king-elect. The goddess would give him a cup of wine if she deemed him a suitable candidate for kingship. But even after the marriage, should she later realise that he was not up to the task of ensuring that the land flourished under his rule, she could repudiate him and accept another in his place. The gift of wine was a recurrent theme in Irish mythic tales associated with royalty. In the 'Tale of Da Derga's Hostel', the luckless King Conaire had a reputation as an unjust ruler, and the story of his death is an interesting take on the withdrawal of the goddess's support for a reign. As a punishment for his parsimony, the druids cast a spell on him, giving him an immense and unquenchable thirst which eventually caused his death. This episode has been interpreted as a symbol of the goddess of sovereignty's denial to him of the sacred cup and her rejection of him as husband and legitimate king.

So what has the theme of wine and sovereignty to do with Wales? As discussed earlier in the book, the Welsh myths are both at a later date (in written form at least) and they are less overtly pagan than the Irish body of material. But dig deep enough, and some remnants of this link between king and goddess might be revealed. For instance, we are told that both Rhiannon and Branwen had reputations for their generosity and their lavish hospitality to the guests who visited their respective courts. When Pwyll, Lord of Dyfed, and his consort Rhian-

DIVINE MARRIAGE
IN ANCIENT ICONOGRAPHY

The indigenous peoples of Roman Britain and Gaul worshipped a myriad of gods and goddesses, as is clearly shown by iconography and epigraphy. Among these images and inscriptions, reference is often made to pairs of deities: male and female. While inscribed dedications indicate that they possessed many different names and personae, it is possible to make tentative links between them and the idea of sacred marriage associated with myths of royal rulership. A good example is a stone relief carving from Gloucester. Although no dedication accompanies the image, it is clear from other epigraphic material from elsewhere that the couple depicted on the Gloucester stone are the Roman god Mercury with his partner, Rosmerta – her Gallo-British name, indicative of a native sobriquet meaning 'the great provider'. The iconography on this stone is complex and fascinating. Mercury looks thoroughly classical, with his usual emblems of a cockerel, winged hat and *caduceus* (a herald's staff entwined with snakes). Rosmerta is wholly Gallo-British in origin, and her status as sovereign is clear from the sceptre she wields. Her role as a giver of prosperity is shown by the stave-bound bucket and ladle that she also holds. The vessel closely resembles buckets used in late Iron Age Britain and Gaul for locally made liquor: mead, fermented berry juice or ale. Rosmerta is depicted in the act of dipping her ladle into the vat as if about to offer Mercury a drink. The Gloucester relief is just one of several similar carved stones from Britain and Gaul. And it suggests that the beliefs it reflects are not dissimilar from the later mythic representation of the divine marriage and the sovereignty goddesses. It is poignant that, as in this case, it is often the god that is identified as belonging to Roman religion while the goddess is a native deity, with her roots in indigenous societies whose own cults were modified to embrace (and adapt to) members of the Roman pantheon. Sometimes inscriptions, too, hint at this kind of merging of religious ethnicities. For instance, a stone from the great temple to Sulis Minerva at Bath is a dedication made by a man called Peregrinus who names himself as belonging to the tribe of the Treveri. The dedication is to Loucetius Mars and Nemetona. Peregrinus twins the identity of Mars with a native god of light, Loucetius. Nemetona's name is, like Rosmerta's, entirely Gallo-British: it contains the Gaulish word *nemeton*, which refers to a sacred grove, a natural place of worship particularly pertinent to Britain and Gaul. So, although cloaked in a cloud of unknowing, these images may have sown the seeds for the sovereignty myths of Wales and Ireland. Rosmerta in particular has so many shared attributes with Rhiannon and Branwen in her provision of plenty.

non rose from their bed on the morning after their nuptials, the first request Rhiannon made to her new husband was not to refuse a gift to anyone who asked for a boon. Soon after, when the couple had arrived at Pwyll's court at Arberth, a great feast was prepared and all the most prominent women and men were invited. Nobody who attended this banquet left the court without being presented with a precious gift, 'either a brooch or a ring or a precious stone'. Interestingly, an almost identical occurrence is recorded in the story of Branwen. As soon as she arrived in Ireland with her husband, Matholwch, all the great and the good of the land gathered to welcome the royal couple. Not one of them who had been presented to the queen departed without 'either a brooch or a ring or a treasured royal jewel'.

It seems to me that these two events are so similar, in terms of the generosity of both women, that what might be chronicled here is a reflection of a lost (or at least faded) sovereignty ritual similar to that which occurred in Ireland. While there was no mention of either woman passing wine to her husband, the symbolism of that ritual may have morphed into the legend of feasting. Prosperity is paramount in both these Welsh tales and it is striking that it was the queens who were renowned for giving the bounty rather than the kings.

A quest tale: 'Culhwch and Olwen'

One of the great Welsh mythic tales tells of a complicated quest undertaken by the young hero, Culhwch, kinsman to Arthur, to find the 'girl of his dreams'. This girl is Olwen, with whom he had fallen in love at the very first mention of her name by his stepmother, and before seeing her for himself. The notion of the quest to find something of great value is by no means unique to this love story. One of the most powerful quest legends is a group of French romances about the Holy Grail, the sacred vessel thought to be the actual cup that held the wine given by Christ to his apostles at the Last Supper. In her book *The Holy Grail: History and Legend*, the folklorist Dr Juliette Wood describes how the medieval writer Chrétien de Troyes, who came from the Champagne region of France, constructed a number of Arthurian romances, of which the most famous was 'The Story of the Grail'. The hero of this story was Percival, a young knight who first saw a jewelled cup in the hands of a maiden at a castle to which he had been invited by an old man. De Troyes probably wrote his tale (which he left unfinished and to be completed by others) in about AD 1180. This mythic story is about the search for and possession of a supernatural treasure – a spiritual gift sent to the world of humans by divine will – but it is an elusive one that had to be won by knightly deeds, hardships and journeys.

Culhwch's quest for Olwen was complicated and difficult. As a kinsman of Arthur, he sought help from him and his knights, all of whom had special, superhuman qualities. Olwen herself is depicted as someone incredibly beautiful, otherworldly and elusive – like the Grail. When Culhwch finally tracked her down to the house of her monstrous father, the giant Ysbaddaden, she appeared before her young suitor like a goddess, white-skinned, yellow-haired and wearing a robe of vivid scarlet silk. She also wore a red-gold torc around her neck – an ornament that signifies the status of a queen or goddess. The ancient Greek writer, Cassius Dio, wrote in similar terms of the great Iceni tribal queen, Boudica, who nearly drove the Roman army out of Britannia in AD 60/61. He emphasised the great gold torc she wore, as an emblem of her rank. I even wonder whether the storyteller – or the cleric who wrote down the tale – was familiar with Dio's historical writings and was, perhaps, influenced by them in his presentation of Olwen. Torcs were also perceived as spiritually charged objects and that is shown by their constant presence in the sacred images of divine beings in late Iron Age and Roman-period Britain and beyond, and by their interment as votive offerings to the gods. One such example is the great hoard of gold torcs carefully buried in pits at Snettisham in Norfolk – an area that would later be Boudica's realm – in the mid-first century BC.

The whole theme of Culhwch's search for Olwen is embodied in the enormous amount of time and manpower it takes to complete. Both Arthur and his knights are involved in fulfilling Ysbaddaden's demands and there was a great deal of investment in completing this quest. The tasks are Herculean, for Olwen's father was, himself, under a kind of curse that meant his death if his daughter wed.

The end of Culhwch's quest and his winning of Olwen's hand occurred when – having gathered the grooming equipment from the boar Twrch Trwyth – the giant's beard was shorn and he was then put, willingly, to death. Culhwch and Olwen consummated their union that night and the tale ends with the statement that 'she was his only wife as long as he lived'. Just like Rhiannon, nothing is mentioned of Olwen's eventual death. Did she die? Or was she, perhaps, immortal?

Women kings? Gender status in sacred marriage

We have explored the relative status of males and females, and have considered whether matches like Rhiannon's union with Pwyll and others might be veiled references to the weddings of sovereignty goddesses with mortal kings, much more explicitly presented in Irish mythic literature. Bearing in mind the culture and society in which the Welsh mythic stories were created and later written down, it would be easy to think in terms of the 'norm', which would have seen the men being of naturally higher rank. But this is too simplistic a view.

I want briefly to refer to the customs and beliefs of another ancient realm: Egypt, land of the pharaohs who were worshipped as gods. One of the Egyptian pharaohs broke the mould of male supremacy – which had already been dented by the frequent marriage between royal brothers and sisters, in order to make the heredity of monarchy doubly strong. In 1479 BC, Hatshepsut, daughter of Amun, took the throne of Egypt, and called herself king. Before this, she first served as regent for her young half-nephew, Thutmose III, and then proclaimed herself ruler alongside him. She reigned as King of Egypt for just over twenty years. Guy de la Bédoyère explains in his book *Pharaohs of the Sun* that depictions of Hatshepsut contained 'all the usual male conventions'. She introduced to her nation the notion that the concepts of a king could be detached from its physical manifestation as a man, and the idea that they could embrace female kingship. In other words, she promoted kingship as a mantle which could be adopted by a man, a woman or conflated as both. Hatshepsut, as a historical figure, embodied both male and female as a legitimate composite of royalty. Interestingly, her images often blurred gender: she was sometimes depicted as a man but her inscribed titles were feminised – although, of course, only the literate (the priests and other members of the elite) could read such titles. I have made this short digression into Egyptology because it serves to explain some subtleties associated with gender status in an ancient society that left a rich abundance of evidence not only for their religious beliefs but also great detail concerning sovereignty.

Wales and its mythic heritage are a very long way from ancient Egypt, both spatially and temporally. However, there is perhaps some mileage in considering a society where gender was not set in stone, at least at the highest layer of rank. Women play a large part in medieval (or earlier) Welsh storylines – not always for good or straightforward, but often meaningful. I find it fascinating that, in Romano-British (and Gallo-Roman) cult imagery, where we see divine partners passing a symbolic cup of sovereignty from the female to the male, the usual pattern of sexual dimorphism – where the male is larger and taller than his partner – is often flouted.

EQUAL PARTNERSHIP IN ROMAN-PERIOD CULT IMAGERY?

I want to return briefly to the carving of the Romano-British divine couple Mercury and Rosmerta found in Gloucester, because it is one of many, in Britain and Gaul, that apparently contradicts the norms of gender dimorphism. Here, Mercury (or the British equivalent) is actually depicted as smaller in stature than his partner, Rosmerta, as if she was the dominant figure. In other iconography, particularly artefacts found in Gaul, divine couples are shown as equivalent in size. One particularly powerful image comes from Sarrebourg in Alsace and depicts a bearded, bare-headed male carrying a small pot and a long-handled hammer. His female partner wears a crown and carries a sceptre in the form of a miniature house mounted on a long pole. The man is presented as older than her, and the sculptor carved them to be of equal height. It is very tempting to interpret such imagery as depicting an equally shared sovereignty or even – like Hatshepsut's version of pharaonic power – as representing a single dual-gendered godhead.

Symbols of sovereignty

It is perhaps fitting that I am writing the final part of this chapter on the day of Queen Elizabeth II's funeral. I was struck by the richness of the symbolism that surrounded this sombre and world-stirring event. The pomp and majesty were breathtakingly moving. The bleakness of mourning a monarch was offset by the splendour of the colour, pageantry and ritual. For me, one of the most poignant elements in the funerary ritual was at Her Majesty's Committal to St George's Chapel, Windsor, where the Lord Chamberlain stepped forward and snapped his hinged staff of office in two, before placing it on the Queen's coffin, where it would accompany her to her final resting place in the royal vault, beside her husband, parents and sister. This, along with the removal of the sceptre, orb and crown from the coffin to the high altar, starkly conveyed the end of a long reign and of an era.

This chapter has been about the symbolism of sacral kingship, the relationship between royal partners and the ceremonial events surrounding monarchy. Feasting played a significant role in Welsh mythic tales of kings and queens, as did gift-giving, splendid garments, feats of honour (and dishonour), fidelity and family. All of these themes came together upon the Queen's death and during her funeral. It was a time of bittersweet imagery that not only displayed the united grief of the royal family, the country and the world beyond, but also revealed tensions and fragilities. Christian belief was writ large in Queen Elizabeth's funerary rituals, whereas its expression was more muted in the myths of Wales, although there is a sense that, despite the magic and wizardry that is sometimes present, God was never far away. Of course, the Christian ethos was almost certainly introduced into the tales by the clerics who wrote these stories down. In their oral form, the tales may have been solidly pagan.

Mythscapes and Deep Roots

*They [the druids] did not want their pupils to rely on the
written word and so neglect to train their memories. For it
does usually happen that if people have the help of written
documents, they do not pay as much attention to learning by
heart, and so let their memories become less efficient.*

Julius Caesar's Gallic Wars translated by Anne and Peter Wiseman

This quotation comes from Julius Caesar's war diaries and specifically
De Bello Gallico ('The Battle for Gaul'). It is important in relation to
the subject of this book because it emphasises the importance of oral
tradition, including storytelling. Tales can be memorised but, if not
written down, they can also be manipulated and changed over long
periods of time while retaining remnants of ancient roots.

To read the Welsh medieval mythic texts is akin to escaping
through C. S. Lewis's wardrobe into the enchanted land of Narnia.
The boundaries of real life, as lived by people, are neither valid nor
necessary in this Never-Never Land. As is true for any dreamlike
mythologies, nothing is too far-fetched to be possible, be it talking

149

A pregnant mouse fears death by hanging, threatened by
Manawydan in revenge for the magic blight upon Dyfed.

heads, shape-changing creatures, wise fish, women made of flowers or wilful cooking pots. The myth-spinners who told these tales and their audiences experienced an otherworld that could be wonderful or weird, fabulous or frightening, and sometimes all of these at once. But myths are not just stories, plucked out of the air by imaginative creators. They often contain grains of truth too. In the Welsh tales we have explored in this book, real events like the introduction of domestic pig-farming and grain-growing, and genuine conflicts – for example between Wales and Ireland – are explained by being woven into the mythic stories.

Throughout this book, I have made frequent reference to the notion that Welsh myths had their roots deep in the past. To my mind, there is sufficient congruence between the archaeological evidence for religious ritual (including divine images) in Iron Age and Roman Britain (and beyond) and certain recurrent themes in the medieval mythic repertoire to argue for suggesting the presence of ancient rootstocks that served to nourish the later stories. Given that the tales themselves had their origins in oral traditions that may have been – like those of Aboriginal Australia – circulating for perhaps more than a millennium, we should not dismiss the possibility that some of the stories were based, or at least fed on, systems that were, themselves, of ancient heritage.

The myths of Wales contain important and persistent connections with Ireland. I think we need to think of the Irish Sea as a highway between Wales and Ireland rather than a barrier. There is a lot of archaeological evidence, some from the Bronze Age and earlier, that craftspeople and merchants exchanged ideas and goods between the two lands. I suspect that storytellers also shared tales and, perhaps, travelled regularly across the sea to perform to both Welsh and Irish audiences. The Irish connection has a strong pulse, partly because of obvious associations like the marriage between Branwen of Harlech and the Irish king Matholwch, and the war that resulted from that, and partly because of shared themes, such as the magic cauldrons, of Irish origin that appear in the Welsh stories. Other storylines that we've explored here confirm this close link. What is interesting, though, is the significant difference between Welsh and Irish mythology: the presence, albeit muted, of the Christian God in the former, and its absence in the latter. I suspect that this is partly due to chronology, as the Irish branch of myth dates from earlier times, not least in its written form, than the Welsh. By the time the Welsh tales were committed to written form, Christianity may have had a stronger hold on the stories, and that would explain why – even in the most pagan themes, such as shape-shifting – God had a voice.

I want to draw attention to something that I don't think has been explored before: the possible role of the druids, that powerful and influential priesthood that dominated the dissemination of trad-ition and religion in ancient Britannia and throughout the lands of its Gaulish neighbours, and with whom my previous book, *Rethinking the Ancient Druids*, was concerned. That the druids, who flourished during the later first millennium BC and the earlier first millennium AD, were linked to mythic stories is strongly hinted at by a particular form of evidence: coins. As was, and is still, true for many coinage systems, Iron Age (and Roman-period) rulers used coins not simply as money but, sometimes more importantly, as a means of conveying information to the masses. Gold and silver coins, in particular, were vehicles for the display and circulation of a rich and complex iconog-raphy that produced propaganda concerning tribes and their leaders, but which also contained messages associated with religious rituals and the gods. It has long been recognised that coin iconography may have been governed by druidic influence.

This is not the right stage for expanding on the evidence for how druidism worked but, if we believe Julius Caesar's testimony, the druidic orders in Britain and Gaul enjoyed a supremacy in tribal and international matters as influential as that enjoyed by the tribal leaders. Indeed, it should be remembered that sometimes the roles of ruler and druid were combined, as in the case of Caesar's friend and ally, Divici-acus, king of the Gallic tribe, the Aedui. It is my belief, and I am not alone in this, that Iron Age coins, with their complicated iconograph-ical repertoire, may well have been used for the circulation of ancient mythologies, some of which chime with elements contained in the Welsh tales explored in this volume. For instance, there is a silver coin from Norfolk that reminds me irresistibly of Twrch Trwyth, the great enchanted man-boar at the centre of the tale of 'Culhwch and Olwen'. Its obverse (front) bears an image of a moustached human head in profile, wearing what appears to be a headdress made of boarskin. Could it, instead of being a human in a headdress, represent a person in the process of shape-shifting between human and wild boar? The inscription on another, alas unprovenanced, British silver Iron Age coin bears a significant message. On its reverse side is an image of a chunky boar, with erect dorsal bristles, as if in fighting mode. But it is the coin's legend that hints loudly at a ritual – perhaps a druidic – presence. At the top is the word 'Tascio', a reference to King Tasciovanus, ruler of the Catuvellauni, whose territory was centred in Essex. Below is the word DI[AS], which has been interpreted as an abbreviation of 'diassu', which refers to a chief priest or perhaps a druid. Other eastern coins bolster this reading, for they depict a *lituus*, a sacred staff used in prophetic rituals. My foray into the iconographical references to ritual and myth on Iron Age coinage must necessarily be brief. But I hope that it serves to validate my tentative suggestion that ancient coins may contain some seeds of old cosmologies – a sort of communication from the druids, whose messages might have already circulated, not just through coin circulation, but also through storytelling.

It is interesting that at least two recurrent themes writ large in the Welsh stories are depicted on Iron Age coinage: boars and ears of corn. At the beginning of this chapter, I mentioned the idea of the Welsh tales containing origin stories associated with the introduction of farming into the country. Readers will recall that in the Third and Fourth Branches of the *Mabinogi*, respectively, reference is made to Manawydan's cultivation of wheat and the gift that the otherworld lord, Arawn, made to Pryderi of Dyfed of the enchanted pigs. These two events can be seen as origin stories for the start of both pig-farming and wheat-growing in Wales.

The theme of opaque and misty references to druids in Welsh mythic tales can be explored a little further. There is very little direct mention of them but there is a story, contained within 'The Tale of Taliesin', that specifically alludes to people called *Derwedd*, which translates as 'oak seekers'. And, remember, in the Fourth Branch, the importance of the oak tree to which Lleu, transformed into an eagle after Blodeuwedd's lover's attack on him, flew for shelter? The word 'druid' is generally accepted as deriving from 'dru' which (in an old Celtic language) can mean 'oak' or 'wisdom'. The ancient place name of *Drunemeton* which was in Galatia (part of Turkey), an area settled by a splinter group of Gauls in the third century BC, literally means 'the sacred grove of the druids'. And we have the Roman writer Pliny's famous testimony to a druidic sacred ceremony in which druids cut down mistletoe growing on sacred oaks on the sixth day of the moon's cycle, when they sacrificed white bulls and prayed for healing and fertility for their people. I wonder if the forest, in which Pwyll of Dyfed went hunting and encountered Arawn, was also full of oak trees. And could it be that the ancient druids themselves morphed into the magicians – Math, Gwydion and Manawydan – who stalked through so many of the Welsh mythic tales?

Whatever the whys and wherefores of the Welsh mythic tales, they are an incredibly rich mine of imaginative storytelling that must have kept audiences enthralled as they listened to them. I can see the story spinners now, enchanting groups of people huddled round a fire at night, their faces lit up by the light of the flames. As these storytellers travelled from court to court or village to village – adjusting the details of their tales to suit their locations, so they were shot through with meaning that made sense to listeners in that particular audience – they shared the magic that belonged to a universal and wonderful world of dreams.

Further Reading

*

All the quotations at the start of Chapters 1–8 are taken from the following translation:

Jones, Gwyn and Jones, Thomas, *The Mabinogion* (London: J.M. Dent, 1976).

The quotation at the start of Afterglow is taken from a translation of Julius Caesar's *Gallic Wars*:

Wiseman, Anne and Wiseman, Peter, *Julius Caesar: The Battle for Gaul: A New Illustrated Translation* (London: Chatto and Windus, 1980).

Books that I can recommend to those readers who have enjoyed *Enchanted Wales* and would like to delve further into the subject:

Aldhouse-Green, Miranda, *Celtic Myths: A Guide to the Ancient Gods and Legends* (London: Thames and Hudson, 2015).

Aldhouse-Green, Miranda and Howell, Ray, *Celtic Wales* (Cardiff: University of Wales Press, 2017).

Davies, Sioned, *The Mabinogion: The Great Medieval Celtic Tales: A New Translation* (Oxford: Oxford University Press, 2007).

Green, Miranda, *The Gods of the Celts* (Stroud: Alan Sutton, 1986).

Green, Miranda, *Dictionary of Celtic Myth and Legend* (London: Thames and Hudson, 1992).

MacCana, Proinsias, *Celtic Mythology* (London: Newnes, 1983).

Redknap, Mark, *The Christian Celts: Treasures of Late Celtic Wales* (Cardiff: National Museum of Wales, 1991).

Williams, Mark, *The Celtic Myths that Shape the Way we Think* (London: Thames and Hudson, 2021).

Wood, Juliette, *The Holy Grail: History and Legend* (Cardiff: University of Wales Press, 2012).

Acknowledgements

I wish to express my gratitude to all the staff at University of Wales Press/ Calon, who have contributed so much to the fruition of this book with their warmth, skill and patience, and who have made *Enchanted Wales* such a pleasure to write. In particular, I would like to thank my editors, Amy Feldman and Abbie Headon, my copyeditor, Caroline Goldsmith, and my proofreader, Anna Baildon, for their meticulous scrutiny and for their wise, friendly counsel. Thanks, Jacob, for your marvellous illustrations.

At a personal level, I need to mention my two Burmese feline familiars, Cassandra and Achilles, who have been with me every step of the way. Their editorial efforts on my computer, not always welcomed, are nonetheless appreciated for their humour value. As always, my human family, Elisabeth, Lily and John, have been wonderfully supportive.

Thank you all.

About the Author

Miranda Aldhouse-Green is Professor Emeritus at Cardiff University. She is the author of *The Celtic Myths*, *Dictionary of Celtic Myth and Legend*, *Exploring the World of the Druids* and, with Stephen Aldhouse-Green, *The Quest for the Shaman*. She was awarded the 2016 Book of the Year Award in the Popular Category by the Society for American Archaeology, and the 2017 Felicia Holton Book Award by the Archaeological Institute of America for *Bog Bodies Uncovered*.

A former President of the Prehistoric Society, Professor Aldhouse-Green was the first recipient of the John Legonna Celtic Research Prize, awarded by the National Library of Wales in 1986. Her international honours include invitations to deliver the Kroon Lecture at the University of Amsterdam in 2004 and the Biennial John Mulvaney Lecture at the Australian National University in 2012. Additionally, she has lectured at academic institutions including the Smithsonian Institution and the Universities of Toronto, Melbourne, Utrecht and Umeå.